WOODBURNING

The Greener Way to Fuel your Home

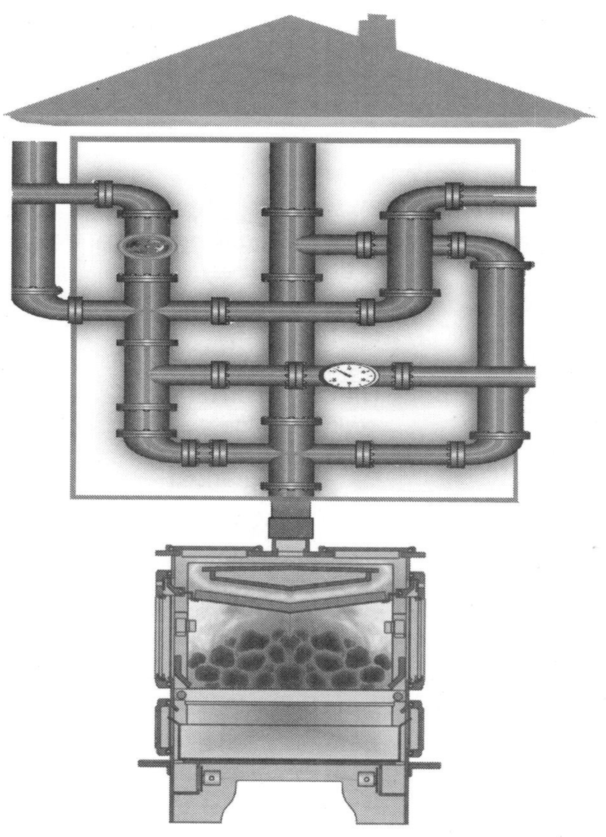

By John Butterworth

Woodburning
Published by The Good Life Press Ltd. 2010

ISBN 978 1 90487 1743

A catalogue record for this book is available from the British Library.

Published by
The Good Life Press Ltd.
The Old Pigsties
Clifton Fields
Lytham Road
Preston
PR4 0XG

www.goodlifepress.co.uk
www.homefarmer.co.uk

Cover design by Rachel Gledhill

Printed in the UK by CPI William Clowes
Beccles NR34 7TL

Contents

An Introduction

We all need energy, and in the West we use lots of it. How else would we keep warm in the UK with our climate? The trouble is, there are millions of us, and our main source of energy is stuff that was buried eons ago, so-called 'fossil fuel'; when we burn that, we release carbon dioxide first trapped many millions of years ago into our atmosphere, and we play our part in adding to the 'greenhouse gases' that are inexorably altering the global climate.

Not only that, fossil fuels are expensive.

So, whether we're keen on saving the world, or we're keen on saving some money, or, as in my own case both - what can we do? Lots of things, and most of the ways of reducing our so-called 'carbon footprints' rather handily save us money too. Insulate, don't run a car, don't fly - some of them sound like hair-shirt solutions to me, but woodburning is not one of those. Ever heard anyone say 'we had a cosy night in in front of the gas fire', or 'we sat round the oil boiler and roasted some chestnuts'? No, I thought not. Use wood as a fuel and you can have it all; reduce your carbon footprint, save some money and gosh, even enjoy life a bit more with a classic roaring log fire.

Nothing so crude as an open hearth though; it's far too wasteful. It may look pretty, but most of the energy from the logs goes up the chimney. If you want to know what your options are in this new world of climate change and increasing energy prices, this book is for you. I've covered a bit of the science behind woodburning - for example, what is meant by 'carbon-neutral' when we refer to woodburning and exactly how much of the world are we saving when we revert to wood fuels (maybe that's a slight exaggeration, but I'll explain exactly how much carbon dioxide is locked into a kilogram of tree, and how it got there).

The options are perhaps wider than you might think, too - there are four types of woodfuel for a start, and many different designs of stove and boiler to burn them on. Then there's the heating system as a whole - you can start with a simple woodstove burning a few logs in one room of your cottage and go up to a huge batch boiler heating all the buildings on your grand estate (not forgetting your swimming pool) - and everything in between. Can you integrate a wood fueled boiler with an existing fossil fueled boiler? Yes you can, even if your plumber shakes his head in denial.

How on earth can you tell how the price of wood fuel compares to fossil fuels such as gas though? You can look at your gas bill for the latter - maybe you'll need to use a calculator, but in there somewhere is the 'price per kWh' and even the total amount you've used over the year, all in black and white. Look at the offerings from log sellers and you'll see logs offered at, say, '£50 per load', which is no different to the energy companies advertising 'some gas' for £50. Chapter 2 will show you how to decipher this ridiculous measure of 'the load' and compare prices per kWh at last.

If you like the idea of wielding manly power tools, we'll take a look at chainsaws, splitters and the like. If you don't, and just want very clean, never seen fuel - there's an option for that too, in the form of wood pellets.

How about growing your own? That's my ideal. That's taking 'renewables' to its obvious conclusion; not only do you use it as fuel, you grow it yourself! And forget the old saying that 'you're planting for future generations', it's rubbish - they'll surely benefit, but in the meantime so will you. Short-rotation coppice is quite close to instant gratification; even planting with long-term woodland in mind will produce thinnings (firewood!) in five or six years, and the wildlife will love you for it. See Chapter 3.

Lastly, you may have heard a lot about the Government wishing to encourage us, the people, to use renewable energy. No doubt there will be more of the 'stick' approach in the form of increasing taxes on fossil fuels, but there's also the 'carrot' of subsidies and loans. Whatever the ethical issues of these ('Taxpayers to Fund Incentives for the Rich', bleat the headlines), they are for each of us to work out. I've restricted my consideration to looking at how we might get our hands on it.

Does it matter whether you 'believe' in climate change or not to become a woodburner? Not at all. The facts and figures that you need to consider before using wood as a fuel are all laid out for you to reach your own conclusions about woodburning as an end in itself.

One thing is certain though; you won't be making things any worse!

John Butterworth 2010

CHAPTER ONE

A Little Science

Why bother with the science? As a woodburner, you'll be doing your bit to alleviate Climate Change, and rather than just using the words 'I'm carbon neutral' and hoping no-one calls your bluff, I've tried to explain exactly why you can rightly make that claim, and more to the point, why it matters. When you meet a 'climate change sceptic', you can hit them with some facts from this chapter. Or just hit them with the book, which is a little heavier.

This is the only part of the book which extolls the many virtues of trees though; the rest explains the most efficient ways to burn them...

What Wood Is

Wood is - what? I thought I knew, but I didn't when it came to it, apart from the fact that it contains a lot of carbon. I do now though, so let's consider it in a little detail. A tree by weight is mostly wood, and if you cut down a deciduous tree in winter when the leaves have dropped, wood is pretty well all you'll finish up with, but what is that material?

It is cellulose and hemicellulose fibres bound together by lignin (I'll cover what they all are later), plus water, plus trace elements and minerals: that's what wood is. As far as the tree as a whole is concerned, wood is the strong 'frame' of a complex living plant, the structure that draws water (plus a few nutrients) from the ground and pumps it up to the leaves that it supports high in the air, where they can get the most benefit from the sun.

The two basic types are 'hardwoods' (trees such as Ash, Oak and Beech) and 'softwoods' (trees such as Larch, Fir and Cedar), and the cell structures are rather different in the two types. The basics remain the same though - take a cross-section through a tree and you'll find, from the centre outwards:

Cross section of a trunk

- The 'heartwood', comprising the oldest cells of the tree that have ceased to function in that they will no longer transport water. This is the toughest part of the tree, and acts as a strong solid core. There's more heartwood in the photograph than in the diagram - it varies from tree to tree, and species to species.
- The 'sapwood', which as you might expect consists of active cells that transport sap (the fluid in cells; nutrients and sugars, but mostly water); the sapwood also acts as a food store for the tree. Together with the heartwood, the sapwood gives the tree its mechanical strength - it's very much 'dual function'.
- The 'cambium' comes next, the thin dark layer covering the sapwood. This is a layer of specialist cells which, when the tree is actually growing, divide to produce new sapwood cells on the inner layer, and new 'inner bark' cells on the outer layer. Where growth

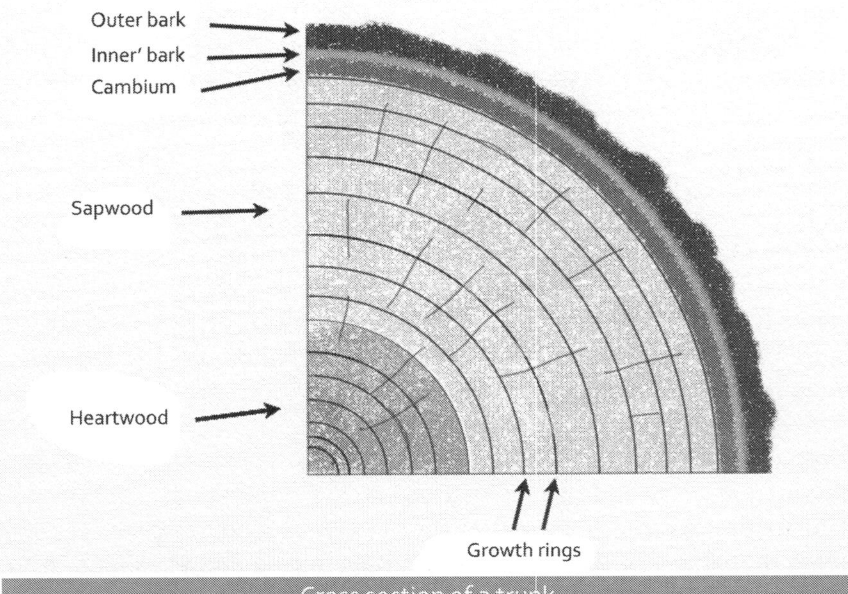

Cross section of a trunk

is seasonal, in 'temperate' regions such as Europe and North America, the new sapwood cells produced by the cambium layer can be identified as distinct 'rings' on the tree. In tropical regions the continuous growth means no tree rings, so a felled tree can't be aged in this way in these regions.

- The 'inner bark' is the part of the tree that moves food (in solution) from the leaves to all other parts of the tree - this food generates new growth.
- The 'outer bark' is the protective layer round the outside of the tree, so it's the bit that you can normally see.

So there you have a slice of wood in cross-section, and an idea of what the distinct layers do. Let's take a look at an entire tree now and consider how that works as a living entity.

The Botany of Trees

Here's a nice simplified diagram of a tree as a living system. Granted, it

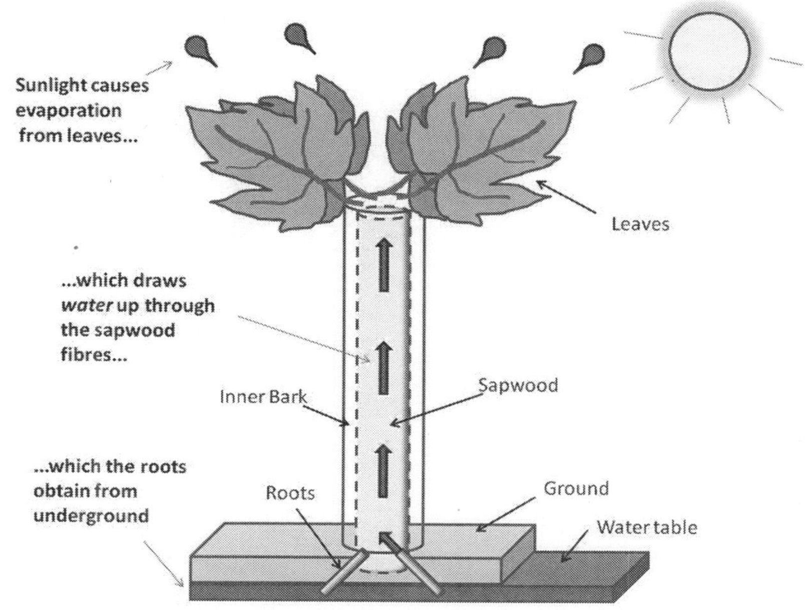

How a tree gets water

only has four leaves, two roots and a couple of tubes for a trunk, but the basics are there. The tree needs three major things to survive and grow - water, sunlight and carbon dioxide from the atmosphere. Water first - as represented in the diagram on page 9.

The tree can't actually pump water, but needs water to get to the leaves somehow - it does this by means of evaporation and capillary action. Water evaporates off the leaves, which draws water up through the long thin hollow cellulose fibres in the sapwood. This in turn draws water from the roots, which have tiny root hairs in the soil where the water is.

So they can access the water and sunlight they tend to grow higher than other plants and spread a leaf canopy to catch as much sun as they can, often at the expense of other trees and plants. But what do they do with the sun and the water?

They use it as part of the process of photosynthesis, which as the name implies, is creating or 'synthesising' something using sunlight (the 'photo' bit). So we have sunlight energy on the one hand, water on the other, and carbon dioxide in the atmosphere all around, and it's the CARBON out of the carbon dioxide that the leaves are after.

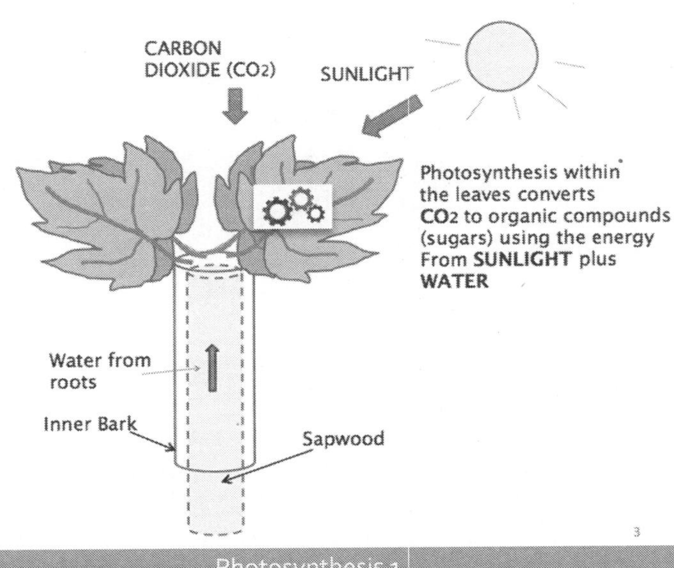

Photosynthesis 1

The leaves absorb CO_2, then use the water and the sunlight energy to convert it into sugars - the leaves act like little factories (hence the cogs in the illustrations!).

Leaves look green to us, incidentally, because green is the part of the visible light spectrum that they reflect as it's pretty much useless to them. They prefer red and violet-blue light as there's more energy in it, so they absorb much more of that.

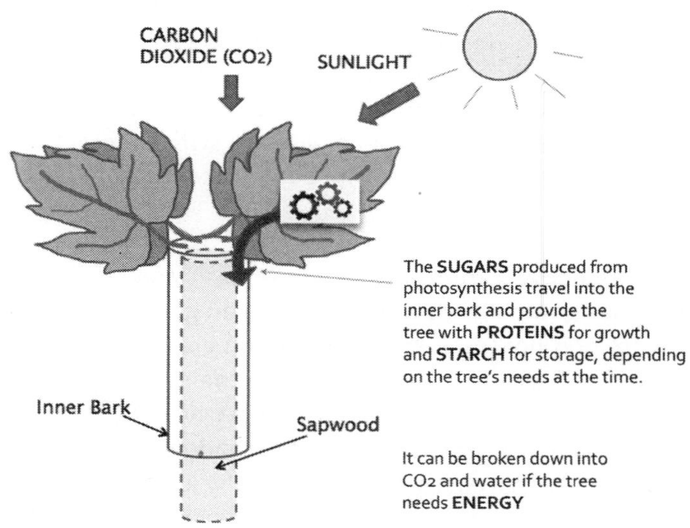

Photosynthesis 2

Once the leaves have produced the sugars (there are several types, but the main one is called 'monosaccharide sugar', or more commonly glucose), it's drawn into the inner bark for distribution through the branches and down the tree. It has three main uses - some is converted to starch for storage; some into proteins for growth and when the sun isn't shining, some is converted back into water and CO_2 for energy production. All three have one purpose; the survival and growth of the tree.

The air we breath is almost entirely composed of two gases; oxygen, about 21%, and nitrogen, almost 79%, plus a very small amount of carbon dioxide. In fact, it's such a small amount it is normally referred to as a 'trace gas', but it is very important to plant life, as we can see. The carbon dioxide gas part of the air is made up of one carbon atom and two oxygen atoms, hence 'CO_2'. All the tree is interested in at this point is the carbon atom - it needs a lot of these, as it effectively 'builds' itself out of carbon. Compress wood for millions of years and you get coal - compress that and you get diamonds. Carbon is just carbon, if progressively more expensive.

A waste product, as far as the tree is concerned, is oxygen. Given that that's the stuff we breath, it's hardly a waste product from the human perspective; in fact, it's photosynthesising plants, along with phytoplankton in the oceans working in a similar way, that maintain the oxygen levels in the atmosphere to the level that supports us, and indeed virtually all forms of animal life on Earth. No great coincidence, just ecology and evolution in action, but another reason for us not to fell the rainforests.

Knowing the above can explain a few things - trees need sunlight for photosynthesis, and if they grow tall they can get more of it. If this is at the expense of other trees, these latter don't grow so well. Trees arrange their leaves as best they can to maximise the sunlight reaching them - this is called 'leaf mosaic'. Beech trees are particularly successful at this, which explains why they cast such dense shadows, and why little grows at the base of beech trees. It also explains why leaves appear to track the sunshine - they are trying to maximise the light that falls perpendicular to the leaf as they can absorb more that way.

Think of leaves as containing little solar panels and batteries to catch and store sunlight - those would be the 'chloroplasts' within the leaf cells. They also have little motors to use that stored power to build more tree - the 'mitochondria' within the leaf cells.

An aside on sunlight and photosynthesis - how can you tell if a far distant planet has green plants growing on it, given that all you can see with the most powerful telescopes today is a speck of light? The 'red edge', that's how. More than half of the heat energy in sunlight is infrared (a slightly lower wavelength than visible red light), and if plant leaves absorbed that energy they would be frazzled, so they have evolved to be strongly reflective of infrared light. This gives a characteristic 'peak' of energy in the infrared part of the spectrum of light reflected from a vegetated planet, so we know to head there on the Starship Enterprise. It's life, Jim, and probably much as we know it.

What is the Material of the Tree?

It's all very well stating that photosynthesis takes light energy and CO_2 and converts it into glucose, but a tree isn't just a sugarlump. The chemical formula for glucose is $C_6H_{12}O_6$, (see also 'the SUMS' below). The tree can modify glucose slightly by removing a single water molecule, ie. H_2O; what's left is $C_6H_{10}O_5$, and these modified molecules like nothing better than to stick together end to end.

Luckily, that's almost all the chemistry you need to know, as $C_6H_{10}O_5$ is the chemical formula for cellulose, and by weight, most of a tree is cellulose and water. Cellulose is a 'polymer', that is a material built up from lots of repeating units of the same thing (modified glucose), and the fact that it's long and thin, stiff and stable makes it ideal for structural use like building tree trunks and branches.

Of course, life is never so simple, and there are two forms of cellulose in wood. The majority, just simple 'cellulose', makes up about 45% of dry wood, and is built up from glucose. The other form, hemicellulose, makes up another 30%, is built up from lots of different sugars and is pretty soft and floppy compared to cellulose. An odd percent or two of dry wood is pectin, the stuff that stiffens jam (or jelly for the Americans).

Cellulose fibres are not strong enough on their own, so there's a third major component of wood, and that's LIGNIN. Think of lignin as a sort of natural plastic that holds the tubes of cellulose together. In a typical softwood tree, say a pine, the wood might be 25 to 30% lignin, and lignin itself is composed of, no surprises here, hydrogen, oxygen and carbon.

Carbon and the 'Carbon Cycle'

Wood is about 45% carbon, and as far as we humans are concerned, carbon is a wonderful element. Element? Yes, if you remember your school science, elements are like the basic building blocks of stuff - add elements together, like say carbon and hydrogen, and you can make complex molecules such as methane. That's CH_4, one carbon atom and 4 Hydrogen atoms. But wonderful? Wonderful because carbon is virtually the only element that sticks to itself and other elements, creating carbon chains and carbon compounds. Imagine it as the basic Lego blocks, and every other element as the fiddly bits like wheels, little model people etc Without the basic building blocks there would be no buildings, so the fiddly bits would be superfluous. We, and all other forms of life on Earth, are built from basic building blocks of carbon - that's how important it is to us. Silicon has similar properties, hence a favourite theme of science fiction writers has been the discovery of 'silicon life-forms', but here on Earth carbon is the basis of all life.

The carbon cycle is often explained with a complex diagram of arrows and boxes, but we're almost there with the simplistic diagrams of my four-leaved tree! We've seen that the tree can pluck carbon from the gases of the atmosphere and convert it into more tree. If animals (including insects) eat parts of the tree, they convert 'tree' into 'animal'. These animals then breathe and give off carbon dioxide gas, which trees use to build more tree. Once these animals have breathed their last and died (expired!), their bodies are broken down by smaller beasties (so-called 'decay organisms') which give off - carbon dioxide of course. More potential tree.

Opposite is the carbon cycle in pictorial form. As you can see, the plants and animals in the diagram, (including those in the sea), respire, and when they do they give off carbon dioxide which adds to the pool of CO_2 in the atmosphere. When plants photosynthesise, both my tree in the centre of the diagram and those sea plants and algae (invisible in my diagram), absorb CO_2. The whole cycle has been in a rough balance for the past 800,000 years or so, meaning that the amount produced was the same as the amount absorbed.

But what about that factory, I hear you say, which of course represents human activity? There's the rub; we humans have done a unique thing in that we've tapped into the Earth's stored carbon, captured from an atmosphere that the dinosaurs were breathing 300 million years ago (the 'Carboniferous Period'; ie. when carbon was laid down as coal).

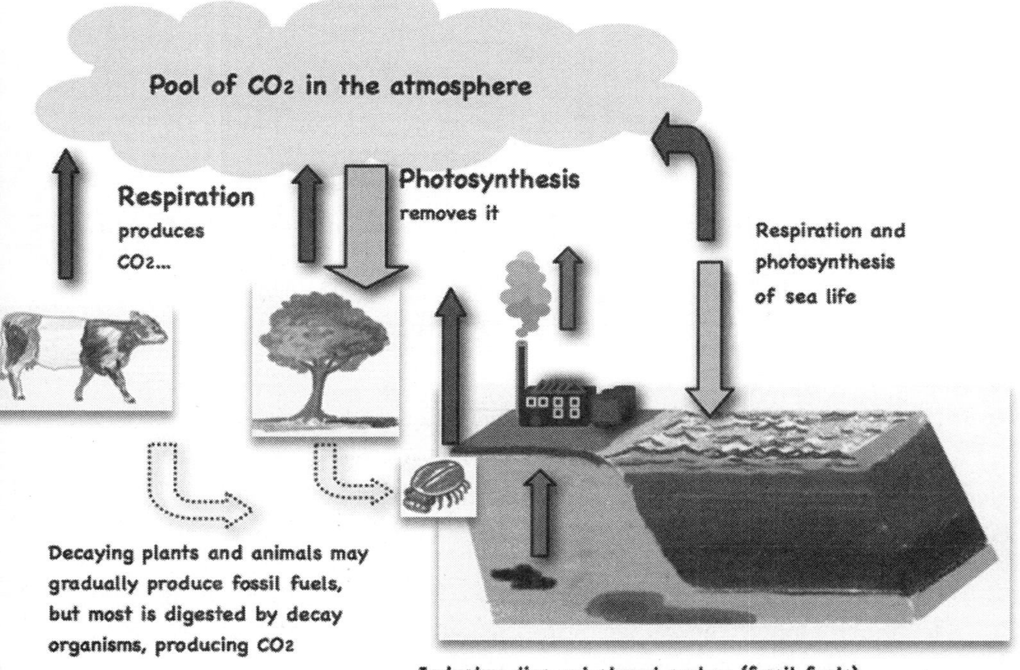

The Carbon Cycle

We mine the coal and pump the oil (oil is found in 600 million year old rock, but I can't find a straight answer to how old the actual oil is!) and corresponding gas deposits, and we burn them. Not only that, we also deforest the land in a massive way. These activities liberate carbon dioxide and upset the 'balance' of the cycle. Suddenly more is being produced than is being absorbed. The amount seems trivial in the scheme of things - there is a colossal amount of carbon dioxide flowing round the cycle. Some 800 billion tonnes is emitted and absorbed each year, and we add to that a measly 27 billion tonnes. The fact that this is a relatively small amount is often used by the 'climate change sceptics' to misrepresent its importance.

What difference can it make to this gigantic carbon cycle? A lot, is the answer. Imagine a perfectly balanced see-saw with a colossally fat person on either end and a hungry crocodile waiting below each one.

One of them is handed a pie - a very small amount of material relative to that person, but more than enough to convince him now that even a tiny addition will upset any delicate balance (and please the crocodile at that end). And we're relentless with our additions; we add more CO_2 every year and have been doing so now for the last 200 years.

The Earth has taken eons to reach the current balance, or at least what was formerly a balance, and indeed it has been accommodating enough to absorb some of our 'extra' carbon. We've disturbed the equilibrium now, and we are continuing to do so. Our crocodile is waiting.

To get a little more perspective, most of the carbon on Earth is effectively trapped in a 'reservoir' within the rocks and sediment, but it stays put and is not even counted in the 'carbon cycle' flows - its so-called 'residence time' is so long that it effectively makes no difference, so the stuff we see 'flowing' in the carbon cycle is just the short-term stuff.

The bad news is that some of that reservoir of material may not stay put for much longer. There's far more carbon in the dead organic material than there is in the living; it's primarily humus and humus-related material in the soil. A panic, though not enough of one, has ensued in recent years in the realisation that if the permafrost regions thaw out, micro-organisms will get to work on the humus and peat and much of that trapped carbon will be released into the atmosphere.

The Greenhouse Effect

When we release extra carbon into the atmosphere in the form of carbon dioxide, a curious thing happens. Light from the sun - we're familiar with the 'visible spectrum' in the colours of the rainbow - passes through the Earth's atmosphere and hits the surface, warming it up. This heat radiates back towards the sky, but it's now slightly lower in frequency as 'infra-red' energy - it's still a form of light energy, but can only be seen with infra-red cameras. Some gases, including CO_2, absorb infra-red really well, and re-radiate it in all directions. This means that the Earth gets a lot of it back, and gets warmer still, almost as if the atmosphere was reflecting it down like a glass roof.

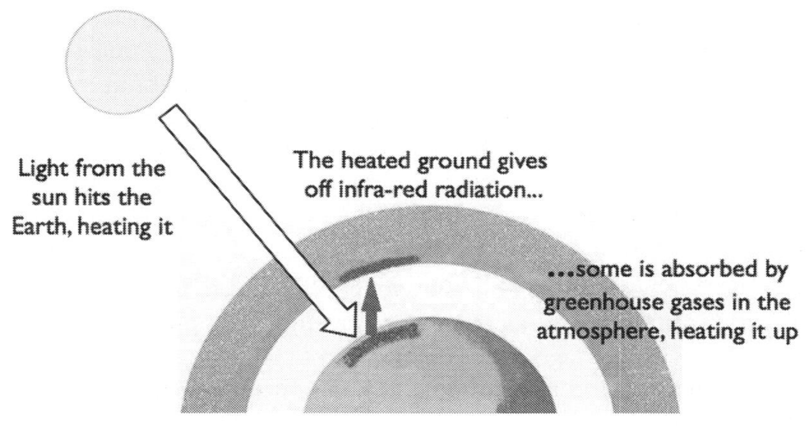

The Greenhouse Effect

That's why it's called a 'greenhouse gas' - there are other, 'worse' greenhouse gases such as methane and ozone, but there is much more CO_2 in the atmosphere, so overall it contributes much more to the greenhouse effect.

Trees and their Part in Climate Change

Now we're getting to the crux of things, ie. why woodburning is generally a good thing, in that it can be done in a 'carbon neutral' way.

When a tree grows it uses carbon dioxide from the atmosphere as its source of carbon; that's the only way it can obtain carbon. A full-grown tree, say a beech tree, is 45% carbon and weighs many tonnes. All this carbon comes from what we humans describe as a 'trace gas'. In fact this 'trace' is so small it's quantified in parts per million of the total gases in the atmosphere - it's defined as the number of molecules of CO_2 divided by the total number of dry air molecules multiplied by one million.

It's a tiny amount - in percentage terms a mere 0.039% of the total volume of gas in the atmosphere - but that percentage is growing at an unprecedented rate. A US scientist called Dave Keeling started measuring the ppm of CO_2 in the atmosphere in 1958 (presumably in the fullness of time we'll hail him as the scientific hero that he is). The longest uninterrupted sequence of readings is from Hawaii, taken at the Mauna Loa Observatory. Back then it was about 311 ppm, but the rising trend was so obvious it was detectable after only about 2 years of data; so by 1960, (source: American Institute of Physics) there was good scientific evidence to show that atmospheric carbon dioxide was on the rise. Consider that when the sillier newspapers say the 'evidence is not conclusive'.

The trend has been inexorable. Between 1958 and today (2010), CO_2 in the Earth's atmosphere has risen from around 311 ppm to around 390 ppm, a rise in percentage terms of 18%. To put that in context, according to ice cores extracted at the Poles, it has not been so high in the last 800,000 years.

How Much of the Tree is Carbon?

We know the relative atomic masses (see below) of carbon (12), hydrogen (1) and oxygen (16), so we can calculate the percentage of each by weight in the cellulose of a tree. For $C_6H_{10}O_5$ the relative weights must be (12 x 6) and (1 x 10) and (5 x 16), that is 72, 10 and 80 of carbon, hydrogen and oxygen respectively. As percentages, 44% carbon, 6% hydrogen, 50% oxygen. Because there's other stuff in a tree besides cellulose, it's generally accepted that the carbon percentage is more like 45%.

The Amount of Carbon in Wood

(The sums; avoid if faint of heart)

The role of trees in the carbon cycle is critical because of the sheer volume of carbon that a tree can capture. There's a chemical equation that goes as follows:

$$6\ CO_2 + 6\ H^2O + \text{sunlight} \text{ -----> } C_6H_{12}O_6 + 6\ O_2$$

...or in plain English, 6 carbon dioxide molecules + 6 water molecules + sunlight gets converted to a complicated sugar (glucose) + 6 oxygen gas molecules. That's the process of photosynthesis written out as a chemical formula.

To work out what that means in kilograms of carbon dioxide, all we need to know is the relative masses of the two types of atom involved, and that these are measured in 'Atomic Mass Units' (1 AMU is the weight of a hydrogen atom, which is our reference point). Here they are - a carbon atom is 12 AMU; an oxygen atom is 16 AMU. So CO_2 being one carbon atom and two oxygen atoms is 44 AMU in total, whilst C on its own is only 12.

For the purposes of this exercise we don't care exactly what the definition of atomic mass units are - all we're after is the relative masses.

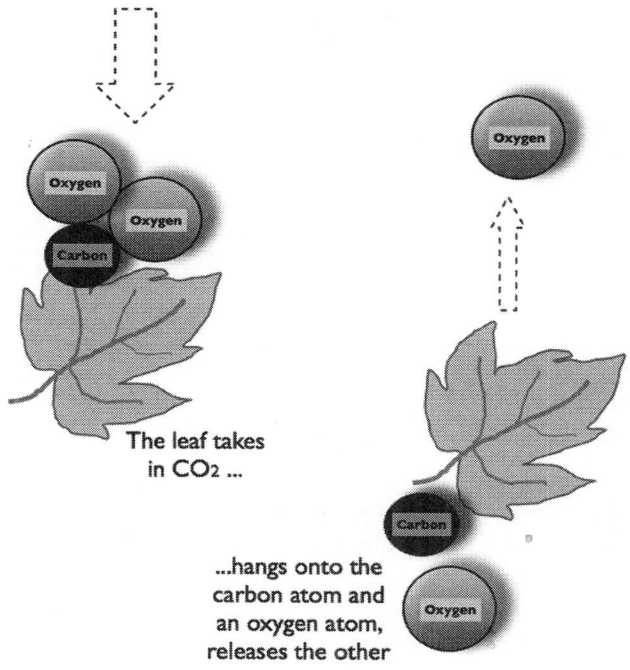

Diagram of leaves converting CO_2 to C and O

The diagram shows this; I've tried to illustrate the relative weights of the carbon and the oxygen atoms. The CO_2 molecular weight is 12 + 16 + 16, that is 44 Atomic Mass Units, whilst the carbon atom that's split off in photosynthesis weighs only 12 AMUs.

(To be pedantic, the single oxygen atoms shown don't stay single, as 'O' on its own is unstable in nature; they always combine with other atoms).

Anyway, because CO_2 is so much heavier than carbon, when CO_2 is converted to carbon by a tree, a lot more CO_2 'disappears' from the atmosphere (in terms of weight) than we'd expect. The 'lost' weight is that of the two oxygen atoms. From a given amount of CO_2, some of the oxygen is converted into the sugar that the tree hangs on to and some is given off by the leaves as oxygen gas; the total weight of the carbon dioxide (44) is converted to carbon (12), and the rest, oxygen (32), is used elsewhere for nice benign activities, so for this sum we can effectively ignore it.

This is called 'carbon sequestration'. It works both ways though - the growing tree takes all the carbon that it needs to grow from CO_2 in the atmosphere; when you and I burn that tree, the carbon recombines with oxygen and re-creates CO_2. No more and no less than it had absorbed - hence we can call it 'carbon neutral'.

Now that we know the relative weights, the sum to calculate the amount of CO_2 converted into carbon is ever so simple - 44/12 in fact, so for every 1kg of carbon sequestrated by the tree, 44/12kg, ie. 3.67kg of CO_2 have been converted.

As a tree is 45% carbon, every 1kg of tree started off as 3.67 x 0.45kg of CO_2, ie. 1.65kg of CO_2. We've ignored the water in the tree here - it's a totally oven-dry tree!

If we knew how much a particular tree weighed, then we'd know how much CO_2 it had captured and converted into tree! Rather than cut down every tree to weigh it, a technique called 'Allometry' has been developed, whereby the mass, or weight of a tree, can be estimated from its diameter in centimetres at a height of 1.4m. The formula, derived from theory and proved by empirical studies (actually measuring the dry mass of loads and loads of felled trees), is $\log_{10}M = -1.25 + 2.66 \log_{10}D$. M is mass in kg, D is diameter in cm. Note that we're still using 'dry' mass, so we're ignoring the water in the tree.

You hardly need to know all that, you may be saying, but now you do you could estimate the weight of your own trees! Let's assume you have a tree with a nice round number, say 40cm diameter at 1.4m from the ground. Using the formula above:

$\log_{10}$ of its mass, M = -1.25 + 2.66 x $\log_{10}$ of 40cm (that is, 40cm diameter).

That works out at $\log_{10}M = -1.25 + 2.66 \times 1.602$ so $\log_{10}M = 3.011$, and M must be about 1.027 tonnes. If we call it a tonne, near enough, that tree must have captured 1.65 tonnes of CO_2 in its life thus far. If you have 100 such trees on your plot, you've captured 165 tonnes of CO_2, so good for you.

There's a tricky number to watch here - where people, often representing some vested interest, state that "humans only release 6 billion tonnes of carbon per year" (usually followed by "so how can we make any difference?"), in terms of CO_2 that equates to 6 x 3.67, or 22 billion tonnes of CO_2. They're quoting the 'carbon' figure deliberately as it's a much smaller number, and they hope we won't notice. As we've seen, every 1 tonne of carbon burned converts to 3.67 tonnes of carbon dioxide.

Combustion

The easiest way of looking at the combustion process is to use a very simple pure hydrocarbon as an example - so not wood then! Methane, that's the fellow, with the nice simple chemical formula CH_4. For every carbon atom there are four hydrogen atoms. Carbon is the 'skeleton' and hydrogen sticks to it (using those sticky bonding sites that carbon has), so even though methane is a gas, it is still a nice, defined hydrocarbon. What happen is this - $CH_4 + 2\ O_2 \rightarrow 2\ H_2O + CO_2$ + Energy.

In plain English methane (the fuel) plus two lots of oxygen (from the air) turn into 2 lots of water + carbon dioxide and energy is given off. Wood burns in a similar way.

Interesting Fact No. 1 - Trees Are Related to Us

There is another good reason to treat trees with respect - they are our relatives. Trees have DNA too, and it's not that dissimilar to human DNA, having the same building blocks with the same bases. Dr Eleanor White, a Canadian natural resources scientist working in British Columbia, has even developed a method of 'DNA matching' for trees with a view to using it in court to convict illegal loggers who fell ancient trees in British Columbian National Parks.

If you find it difficult to come to terms with the fact of the shared ancestry of human beings and primates, which at least look like hairy versions of us, brace yourself now as you consider an even more distant ancestor, a plant! I always thought 'tree huggers' a bit odd, but maybe they're just ancestor worshippers.

Perhaps I'm over-emphasising our relationship a little; it was all a very long time ago, as they say, and the split in Darwin's 'tree of life' between the single-celled organisms that later became plants, and those that became animals and much much later us, occurred about 1.6 billion years ago. However, compare that with the first evidence of life some 3.8 billion years ago and you'll see that we shared a common ancestor for a full half of the whole history of life on Earth.

The first tree to have its genome sequenced, the poplar, has about 45,000 genes compared to 23,000 in a human. That's right, the tree's DNA is more complex than ours, so next time you cut one down, just think of that.

Interesting Fact No. 2 - Why Trees Grow Tall

Why indeed, a good question. All they are trying to do is reproduce, usually in competition with other trees, and to do that they try to extract the maximum energy from sunlight to make them grow big and strong. Ideally, they'd never grow tall, just tall enough to spread a mighty array of leaves far enough off the ground to avoid browsing animals. It's local competition from other trees and plants that makes them grow quite so tall.

Above -Single tree   Below - Competition!

Here's a spreading tree (above) with no competition and some narrow trees (below) with lots of competition. Contrast the way the narrow trees put effort into growing taller to get to the sun, hence producing more trunk, which is just what we want as woodburners. The moral here is grow them close together if you want plenty of wood, thinning out only gradually as they grow. In our wood we grew them for ten years before we even thought about thinning - the tall beeches in the picture are 24 years old.

Looking to the Future: Long - Term Storage of Carbon in Trees

It's common knowledge that ancient trees and peat can become fossilised in the form of coal - if that material is simply left in the ground (in the case of the UK, in a fit of Government pique following the 1984 miners' strike!), then the carbon essentially remains 'trapped' forever. It was captured from ancient carbon dioxide in the distant past, granted, but we've been burning it with great abandon since the start of the Industrial Revolution. The UK might use more gas than coal nowadays - though gas is a fossil fuel and liberates ancient carbon too - but developing nations are increasing the rate at which coal is burned at an unprecedented rate. China, for example, is commissioning the equivalent of one new 500MW coal-burning power station every two and a half days at the time I write this, according to the International Energy Agency. According to the New

York Times, by 2006 China was burning more coal than the EU, the USA and Japan combined.

So globally we're not doing so well on the 'storing carbon in trees' front. How could we do better? Well this book is largely about burning wood on a short cycle, that is, growing trees, chopping them down and burning them, with a view to 'carbon neutrality' rather than actual carbon reduction. They can, or at least could, given the will, be used to stash the stuff away longer term though, in several ways.

- Chop them down and leave them to rot slowly - unlike burning, which releases the carbon immediately, rotting may take twenty years or more to release the carbon stored in the tree. Still very short-term though.

- Chop them down and store the timber in fresh water. What?? According to the University of Missouri Tree Ring Laboratory, trees submerged in fresh water will 'keep' for maybe 2000 years. In fact in northern Missouri the researchers from the Lab have found oaks dating back 14,000 years! It seems like lunacy at first hearing, though remember it's a mad, mad world - and in terms of the wider picture it may be quite logical. As your timber matures, fell it then store the felled trees (I assume nice straight logs, probably just the trunks for maximum stackability) in a fresh-water lake. What do you actually sell then? The 'carbon storage' by the tonne.

- Turn the timber into charcoal and store that. Like storage under water, the idea is to prevent the release of the carbon back into the atmosphere, and charcoal doesn't rot down the same as green wood. Unless you burn the charcoal, the carbon is locked in as effectively as it would be in a pile of unburned coal. A company called 'Carbonscape' was a runner-up in a competition run by the Financial Times in 2009, called 'Climate Change Challenge' - in fact Carbonscape was the judge's choice for winner with a machine they called the 'Black Phantom', a sort of large microwave cooker that can turn both timber and other forms of biomass into nice stable charcoal. Oddly, the FT suggested that such a machine would be 'carbon neutral' even if the charcoal was then burnt as fuel rather than stored, but that's surely not the case - the machine uses energy in the form of electricity to convert the biomass to charcoal. Simple fellow that I am, I'd have thought it more sensible to simply chuck the timber onto your stove and burn it as wood.

- Grow more trees. That's more like it. We always look for complicated solutions, don't we; geo-engineering is all the rage, let's create an artificial tree - forget it! In the immediate future just plant more trees; a real tree is the best way to 'emulate' what a tree does! UK tree cover is 12%, about a third of the the Western European average. A 2009 report 'Combating Climate Change: a Role for UK Forests' detailed no less than four ways that more tree planting would help - number one is that more trees would 'mop up' more greenhouse gases. Number two - we'd be able to burn some as biomass and reduce our dependence on fossil fuels. Number three - use some of this extra timber in the building industry to offset the use of energy-intensive concrete and wooden frames inside houses would lock up carbon for as long as the building existed (that's three and three a) really). Number four - more green space amenity in a crowded country. What, as they say, is there not to like?

Further Reading

The Selfish Gene by Richard Dawkins - in fact, virtually any of Dawkins' books on evolutionary biology.

Combating Climate Change: A Role for UK Forests can be seen on forestry.gov.uk.

Sustainable Energy - Without the Hot Air by David J C MacKay 2009. Free online at withouthothotair.com, or better still, buy a copy for about £20 and worth every penny. David MacKay is a Physics Professor at the University of Cambridge and this is the best book on sustainable energy bar none.

The conversion factors are strangely difficult to obtain as looking for 'carbon sequestration' comes up with all sorts of waffle from contributors with various axes to grind. Put '44/12 CO_2' into a search engine and different methods of explaining the CO_2 to C conversion will appear. Kennesaw State University, Georgia, USA have published a good explanation online. Search for 'ESA21'.

CHAPTER TWO

The Fuel Value of Wood

Virtually all the alternatives to woodfuels are priced per kilowatt-hour (kWh), so for valid comparisons we must be able to convert any amount of any type of woodfuel to price per kWh, whether we bought it by the 'load', the cubic metre or by the tonne. Price per kWh is what I mean by its 'fuel value', and this chapter shows you how to calculate it. It also explains how to calculate your total fuel requirements, so you will know how much room you might need for each type of woodfuel.

Why should you care about the 'fuel value' of your woodfuel? Here are several good reasons:

- Incredibly, in the UK logs are sold by the 'load'. If we can't work out the fuel value, we don't know what we got for our money, and can't even compare one supplier with another!
- Knowing the fuel value will let you compare the true cost of one type of woodfuel against another (is a cubic metre of hardwood logs at £100 better value than a cubic metre of softwood logs at £50? Should I install a pellet stove or a log stove?)
- You may have an alternative energy supply such as gas - you need to know how woodfuel prices compare with it.
- Even if you find a supplier offering a known quantity (such as a cubic metre of logs), is it good value?

You might well ask yourself "why don't I just look at some of the comparison calculators on the internet from suppliers?" They look easy enough to use; you can just type in the current costs of whatever fuel, and out pops a comparison of your chosen woodfuel with, say oil or coal. So why not use one? The blighters are usually wrong, that's why not. There may be a really good one but I couldn't find it, and I looked pretty hard. For a start, most of them start with 'enter the price per tonne of logs', and you'll have to say - "I don't know that - I got 'a load', not a tonne". Don't worry, even if you knew the price per tonne, chances are the calculator will make some basic error. I ended up having to work it out from scratch.

We wouldn't need to do all the following calculations if there were reliable standards in the UK. There are good established standards for woodchip and wood pellets, and there are proposed standards to cover all woodfuels (the 'CEN/TC 335' standards), but until those get ratified and enforced, if you don't know the stuff in this chapter you are at the mercy of 'White Van Man' with his 'load' of logs and none of us want that.

The Vital Graph

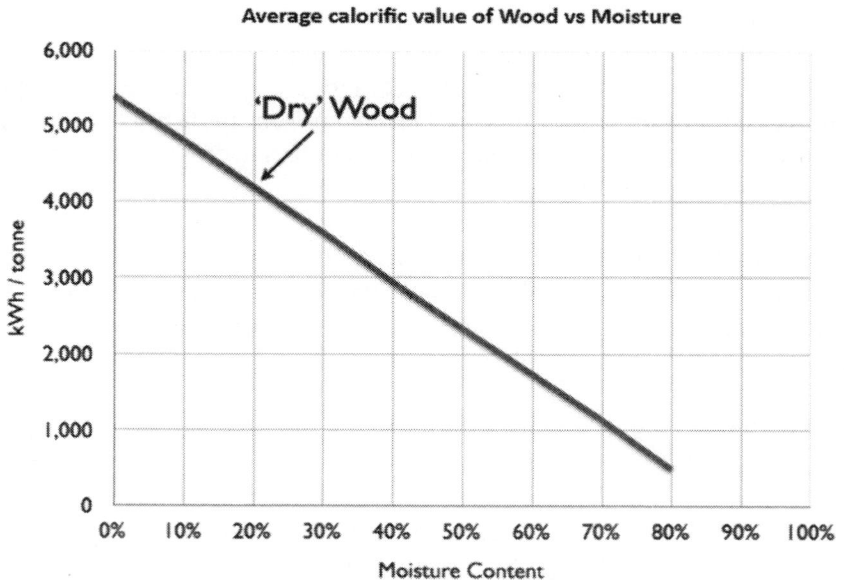

Heating value of wood

Source of data: Biomass Energy Centre and others

We need to understand this vital graph as woodburners as it shows us the light in all this murky talk of 'a load of logs'. It was derived scientifically by drying out wood under controlled conditions, then actually measuring the energy that it gave up in combustion. Virtually all woods are close enough to make no difference in practice, so oven-dry ash has pretty well the same energy content as oven-dry willow, which may come as a surprise (it did to me anyway). I can't find out who originally derived the figures, but versions of this graph appear in most guides.[1]

At one end of the scale 'oven-dry' wood with a zero moisture content (this is called an oven-dry tonne or 'ODT'; theoretically possible, but you can't buy it like that) has an energy content of 5.5kWh/kg. Further down the scale, at about 20% moisture content, we get the term 'dry wood', which is the point that fully seasoned logs reach in a normal temperate climate such as Europe and the US. They seldom get any drier, no matter how long you keep them, so you may as well burn them at that degree of dryness.

Alas for us, there are two potential maximum energy contents for wood - the theoretically perfect one is called the 'upper heating value' (UHV) and that is where the wood is burned and the water vapour formed during combustion is fully utilised (yes, even from perfectly dry wood; it's a 'combustion product' - hydrocarbons contain hydrogen, carbon and oxygen and give off CO_2 and H_2O when burned).

It seldom is fully utilised, certainly not in our normal woodburners, so there's another term called the 'lower heating value' (LHV) where the water vapour isn't used, which reduces the theoretical heating value a bit - about 5%.

LHV is the one we're interested in as that's the 'real life' figure. That's why the graph of energy output versus moisture content doesn't reach 5.5kWh at zero moisture content - it's based on the lower heating value, about 5.3kWh per kilogram, so that's our theoretical maximum figure for perfect woodburning stoves. We'll touch on 'perfect' later. The Government Digest of UK Energy Statistics (DUKES) stats refer to 'net' value - that's the same thing as LHV.

[1] You'll see versions that use 'joules' as a measure of energy - the joule is the amount of energy expended when a force of one Newton is expended over one metre - I could go on for ever here ('What's a Newton then?'), so rather than that, I'll say the conversion factor is 1kWh = 3.6 million joules or MJ. As I want to show you how to compare like with like, I'll only use kilowatts or kilowatt-hours for everything, so no more joules.

To reiterate - when you reach 'oven-dry' conditions, the lower heating value is virtually the same for all woods, even hardwoods and softwoods, as they're similar hydrocarbons - you may think you'd get more heat per kg from hardwood logs but actually it's the other way round. Some softwoods like firs contain 'volatiles' which have their own energy content, so you get a tiny bit more heat per kg than with hardwoods!

Moisture Content of Wood

There's more scope for confusion in the way that 'moisture content' (MC) is quoted. Again there are two 'standards'; moisture content on a 'dry' basis and moisture content on a 'wet' basis.

Moisture content on a DRY basis is the ratio of water based on the ratio to dry wood, so if it's half water and half wood, as much green timber is, then the MC would be 100% (dry basis). Foresters tend to use this ratio.

Moisture content on a WET basis is based on the percentage of water based on the overall weight of timber, so the example above would have an MC of 50% (wet basis).

The bioenergy sector uses MC on a wet basis, and it seems to be quoted in the literature far more than the dry basis, (and common sense tells you that 'wood with a 100% moisture content' sounds like it should be a chunk of water rather than a chunk of wood!) so I'll use WET basis for everything.

The Weight of Logs

For a given VOLUME, hardwoods have a lot more energy than softwood simply because they weigh more; a cubic metre of hardwood logs will weigh more than a cubic metre of softwood logs and more kilograms of wood equals more energy.

So the next vital piece of information for us must be - how much does wood weigh? We'll need that, because in the UK at least, logs are usually sold by volume, not weight, so without it we haven't a clue how much energy we have just bought. Not only that, the moisture content (MC) is generally unknown, so we might be buying (on a wet basis, remember) wood of 30%, 40%, or even 60% MC, in which case 60% by weight of what you just bought is water! Note that both woodchip and pellets are sold by weight in the UK; I'll look at them later.

If we could have a 'standard' to work to, for example weight per cubic metre of oven-dry spruce, ash etc., maybe we could calculate what we actually bought and see if it's good value - for example, perfectly dry spruce weighs about 375kg per solid cubic metre. So the absolute best we'd get with a 100% efficient stove would be 375kg x 5.3kWh per oven-dry kg, which would give us 1988kWh of energy for a cubic metre of that wood.

Life is not like that in practice though. We'll virtually always burn logs at 20% moisture content, so-called 'air-dry', as that's what we'd get with two years of seasoning. At around that point it might even start to re-absorb atmospheric moisture - so without applying external heat we don't have the means to get it any drier than that. If spruce had a 20% moisture content, the same cubic metre would give us less energy than an oven-dry cubic metre. Not only that, we're looking at logs, not solid blocks. So how much less energy?

Table 1 shows the energy content of timbers of different sorts. I've used the average 'dry matter content' for the calculations shown in column two, obtained from a number of sources - as with all things woody, there's a range of values even for one type of wood.

In the third column I've calculated what the weight of a solid cubic metre of each wood would be if 20% of the cube was water; then, given that there's a lot of air between loose logs - about 48% 'log' and the rest is air - I've multiplied that weight by 0.48 to derive the weight of a metre cube of logs at 20% moisture content.

In the fourth column I've looked at the graph and seen that at 20% moisture content wood has an energy value of about 4.1kWh per kg, so I've multiplied my metre cube of logs by 4.1. In the last column I've assumed a typical wood stove or boiler is 80% efficient, so multiplied by 0.8 to give a value for the output of a hypothetical stove.

Type of Wood	Dry Matter Content per m3 for a solid cube (fifs from COFORD ** and others)	Loose logs at 20% moisture, weight per m3	LHV Energy per m3 of logs at 20% moisture, (log weight x 4.1)	LHV Energy per m3 of logs at 20% moisture, 80% efficient stove
Spruce	375 kg	225 kg	**923 kWh**	738 kWh
Pine	460 kg	276 kg	**1132 kWh**	905 kWh
Ash	570 kg	342 kg	**1402 kWh**	1122 kWh
Beech/Oak	580 kg	348 kg	**1427 kWh**	1141 kWh
Birch	510 kg	306 kg	**1255 kWh**	1004 kWh
Poplar	*365 kg*	*219 kg*	***898 kWh***	*718 kWh*
Sycamore	540 kg	324 kg	**1328 kWh**	1063 kWh
Average Hardwood*	550 kg	330 kg	**1355 kWh**	1082 kWh
Average Softwood*	418 kg	250 kg	**1030 kWh**	820 kWh

Table 1 - Energy content of 1m³ of logs

* Figures rounded and omitting poplar, which has a similar energy content to softwoods.

** COFORD is the Irish National Council for Forest Research and Development

Table 1 above shows the detail if you know exactly what you're getting, but very often you won't know beyond 'hardwood' or 'softwood' from the typical UK supplier, so I've worked out the average value of each. Note that I've left out poplar from the 'average hardwoods' calculation as it's more like a softwood when it comes to fuel value!

Example of How this Table Converts VOLUME to ENERGY

Say, as is usual in the barmy, unregulated UK market, you buy loose logs by the 'load' - that can be converted into cubic metres, or m³ as you'll see later. Assume you'll only burn it when it reaches 20% moisture content - It will take up more or less the same volume at 20% as it does when it's fresh green timber as the water merely fills the hollow cells, so unless it's essential that you use it straight away you can ignore the moisture content when you get it and season it yourself. I have to point out though, if storage is an issue and you have to buy it ready for use, you'll pay a premium for 'seasoned logs'.

To work out the energy content of a volume of wood we start from the weight of solid wood per m³.

For SOFTWOODS, taking the example of spruce:

Start with solid, oven-dry cubic metre block of wood eg. Spruce. 375 kg

Add water; 20% of total weight now water 469 kg

Convert to logs, so 48% now wood; rest is airgaps 225 kg

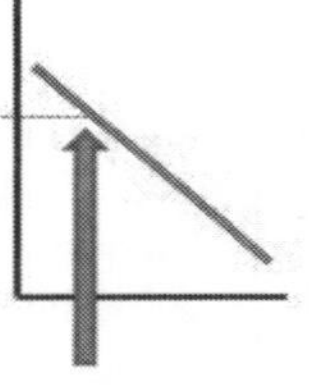

From Graph, 225 kg X 4.1 = 923 kWh

How the numbers were calculated

- A SOLID 1m³ of spruce will weigh about 375kg. There's a range for spruce, but 375kg is about average. That's its weight, or mass, in kg if it was completely bone dry.

- The wood we buy is never bone dry and green logs have maybe 50-60% moisture content, but let's assume that we season it until it contains 20% water as a percentage of its total weight. We work that out by dividing 375 by 0.8, so the wet weight of the solid cube would be 469 kg.

- A cubic metre of loose logs will have a lot of air gaps, so we know we won't get anything like a solid cubic metre of wood. The wood content in a cubic metre of loose logs might be about 48%, taking a view on the range of figures given in the literature, so we multiply by 0.48, which gives 225kg of loose logs.

- Now we refer to the graph - at 20% moisture, the energy output per kg is shown as about 4.1 kWh/kg, so we multiply this mass of logs by 4.1. 225kg of logs therefore has a calorific value, the lower heating value, of 923kWh per m^3.

- Our woodburning stove won't be perfect, so the actual heat we'll get from it will be less than that. At 80% efficiency we'd get 914 x 0.8 or 738kWh from that cubic metre of spruce logs, a fairly typical softwood.

The same calculations for hardwood, lets say ash, that favourite of woodburners everywhere, would give a figure of 1122kWh for a cubic metre of loose logs when burned on an 80% efficient stove.

So you can see, if you can get hold of hardwood logs, for the same volume of loose logs you'd get much more energy from those than from softwoods.

If both cost say £40 for a cubic metre, how would we compare that to the price of gas? The price of your gas is based on the amount of gas coming in through your meter before it gets to your boiler. To compare like with like then we'll have to use the energy from the column on the table before it gets burned on the stove. That's why that column is in bold.

The spruce would really have cost you £40 for a potential 923kWh, that is 4.3p per kWh, whilst the ash would have cost £40 for a potential 1402kWh, that is 2.9p per kWh. Next, from your gas bill, divide the total amount used over the year by the total amount you paid - maybe 4p per kWh.

At last we get to a valid comparison, and you wouldn't believe how long it took me to get there from the learned literature! Finally, these are the figures that you can use to compare the cost of wood with the cost of gas, oil or whatever your alternative heating source might be.

Why bother with the end column you might ask? In Chapter 5 where we consider how to calculate your heat requirement using online calculators, if you come up with a figure of say 18kW for your house, that's the actual amount of output you need from your boiler (ie. you need an 18kW boiler), so you might need to know what the efficiency of your boiler is, as well as the energy content of the logs, to know how much fuel you'll need. I'll come to that again later under the heading 'How Much Power Do you Need?'.

Other Conversion Factors

If you can buy logs as the continentals do, by the stack, the principle remains the same but the conversion factors are different. Remembering that loose logs are about 48% solid mass (so 52% is fresh air) -

- Stacked logs 1m long: 65% solid mass
- Stacked logs 2m long: 60% solid mass
- Stacked logs 3m long: 55% solid mass
- Stacked, sawn and split logs, 33cm long: about 70% solid mass for beech, 80% solid mass for spruce

Source: A Danish publication, 'Purchase and Sale of Wood for Energy Production'.

These figures can be used with Table 1 to convert any volume to energy. So, as an example, if you bought a split and stacked cubic metre of beech, the numbers would be:

580kg as a solid dry cubic metre as before. Add 20% water by total weight, (simply divide 580 by 0.8) giving 725kg. Multiply by 70% now to allow for the fact that there are fewer air gaps in a stack than in loose logs = 508kg of logs at 20% moisture content in the stack.

Multiply by 4.1, the energy in kWh per kg for wood with 20% moisture (from the 'Vital Graph', page 27) - you'd have a calorific value of 2081kWh in that cubic metre, much more than the same volume of loose logs.

For a tight stack of spruce the numbers work out at 1538kWh/m^3, etc. etc.

Calculating the Value of any 'Trailer Load'

I noted that our market for logs in the UK is unregulated - perhaps 'shambolic' would be a better description. As often as not logs are offered by the 'trailer load' or the 'van load' - it's incredible that we'll buy anything on that ridiculous basis, but we do. Anyone willing to buy 'a container full' of petrol for £50? I thought not. The bigger the rogue, the better he likes our inability to compare like with like (try this example - is your mobile phone better value than your neighbour's, and can you find out without recourse to a massive spread sheet?).

All is not lost though. Now that we know how to calculate the energy value of a metre cube of all the common types of log, we can finally calculate the true value of what we're buying.

An example - I got the offer of a 'trailer load' of logs for £35, using my own trailer and picking the logs up from a yard. Was it worth it?

Flat trailer load

The trailer is 2.44m x 1.22m x 0.4m deep, so filled level with the sides it holds 1.19 m^3. Obviously you'd interpret an offer of a trailer load to mean 'as much as you can cram on without it falling off in transit', but how to measure the volume now??

I got it home, took off

the excess and bagged it, to be left with a level trailer load, so I knew that was exactly 1.19m^3. I emptied the trailer, then reloaded the bagged stuff and measured how much space that occupied - 1.22m x 0.6m x 0.4m deep, near as dammit, so that's 0.29m^3. Added together I now know that my trailer load of loose logs is 1.48m^3, near enough 1.5m^3 if I try a bit harder.

So I paid £35 for 1.48m^3. My diesel for the round trip cost me maybe another £3 so I'd better add that, making £38 in total (I'm assuming my time is free - maybe I'd have been lying in a hammock drinking beer instead of collecting logs, which is good healthy exercise). At that rate a single cubic metre has cost £25.68. They were softwood logs, so looking at the Table, good for 1030kWh per m^3, so they cost me 2.5p per kWh. At the time of writing gas cost 3.1p per kWh, so hallelujah, it was worth it.

If you get a 'trailer load' delivered, use a known container to figure out the total volume such as a metre cube dumpy sack, or easier still, calculate the volume of your log store just like I did for my trailer and mark the walls at the level of each cubic metre. If you find that you actually got say 2.5 cubic metres of hardwood logs in a 'trailer load', simply multiply the average hardwood log value from the table (1355kWh/m^3) by 2.5. Divide that into what you paid (say £100) and there you have it - 2.9p per kWh.

The downside of this method is that you won't know if you are going to be happy or ripped off until after the delivery. What you will know is whether or not to use that supplier again.

Simple Rules of Thumb

These rules apply only - and this point is crucial - once the logs are properly seasoned, ie. down to about 20% moisture content:

> 1 cubic metre of loose softwood logs weighs 250kg: energy about 1030 kWh
>
> 1 cubic metre of loose hardwood logs weighs 330kg: energy about 1355 kWh

For 1m lengths stacked very neatly using a conversion factor of 0.65 for both hard and softwood compared to a solid block of wood:

1 cubic metre of 1m long neatly stacked softwood logs weighs 340kg: energy about 1395kWh

1 cubic metre of 1m long neatly stacked hardwood logs weighs 447kg: energy about 1835kWh

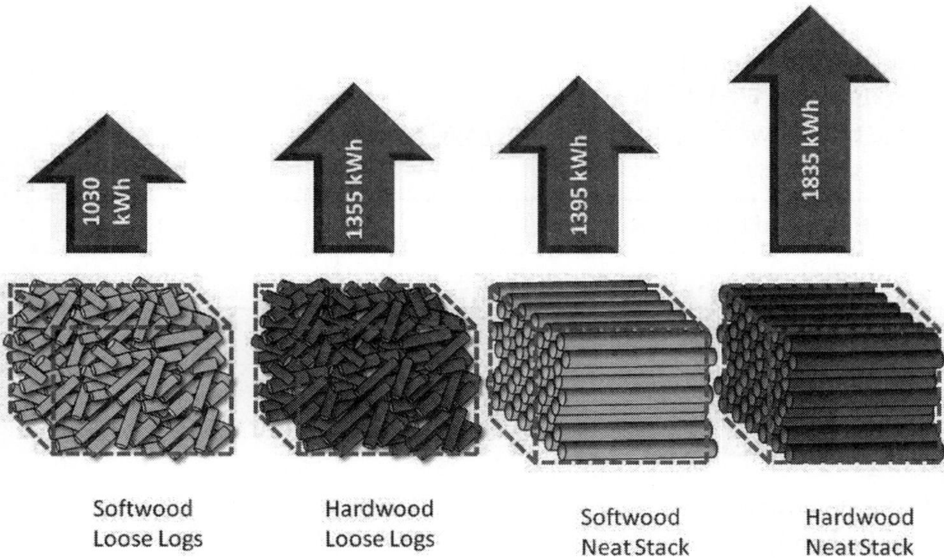

Energy output of logs compared

Calculating 'fuel value' based on a cubic metre is now easy - supplier X is offering seasoned hardwood logs at £120 per m³ (he is too, I just looked him up). Is that good value? Looking at the rule-of-thumb, he's actually selling 1355kWh for £120. That's 8.8p per kWh, which is equivalent to the current price of electricity, the dearest of all the fuels. So no, it's not good value. Shun him.

Buying Woodfuels by Weight

Some woodfuels, wood pellets and woodchip almost inevitably, and sometimes logs, are bought by weight. This makes calculating what we paid in terms of pence per kWh far easier. The moisture content for both woodchip and wood pellets should always be given (don't buy from the supplier that won't tell you!!), so it's simply a matter of looking at the graph for the energy per tonne. I've then derived the volume of the fuel so we can see how much room we might need.

One Tonne Material @ Moisture %	Volume m^3	Energy Content kWh
Loose Softwood Logs / 20%	4	4100
Loose Hardwood Logs / 20%	3	4100
Stacked Softwood Logs / 20%	2.9	4100
Stacked Hardwood Logs / 20%	2.2	4100
Woodchop Softwoods / 25%	5*	3800
Woodchip Hardwoods / 25%	4*	3800
Woodchip Softwoods / 30%	4.8*	3600
Woodchip Hardwoods / 30%	3.8*	3600
Pellets / 8%	1.5	4800
Oil (for comparison) 0%	1.1	11700

Table 2 - Energy content of a tonne of woodfuel

* Bulk densities of woodchip are quite variable; these values are indicative only.

Paid £150 for a tonne of wood pellets? At 4800kWh per tonne you paid 3.1p per kWh.

How Much Power Do You Need?

In Chapter 5 we look at how to calculate your energy requirements from scratch using online calculators. These calculators merely calculate the size of woodstove or boiler that you'll require, but they can't tell you how much fuel it will burn over the course of a year. There are two methods of working out the latter.

One is to use a simplification called the equivalent full load hours (EFLH), a sort of 'rule-of-thumb' that estimates that you'll run your boiler at the equivalent of full load for about 1200 hours per year in a domestic property in the UK. So if you have calculated that you need an 18kW boiler, multiply that by 1200 and you come up with 21,600kWh for the whole year. That's the output power that you need from your boiler though - if it is only 80% efficient you need to add 20% to work out the fuel you'd need to put into it to achieve that. Divide the 21,600 by 0.8 and we see that 27,000kWh of fuel is required.

This second method is more accurate though - you can see how much energy you're currently using from year to year from your energy bills. We'll take town gas as an example as that's the most common by far, but the same principles apply if you use, say heating oil - just see how much you used!

The average UK domestic gas consumption is just over 20,000kWh per year, of which 16,000kWh is for space heating, the rest being water heating (and a tiny bit for cooking). As gas is the most commonly used source of energy for space heating, we'll use that as a starting point.

Anyway, lets assume you are an average user of 20,000kWh of gas per year. Unlike the first method using the EFLH, this 20,000kWh is the total heating value of the gas you bought from the gas company before it got converted to heat by your boiler, so it already takes account of boiler inefficiency. If your gas boiler is 80% efficient you got only 80% of the 20,000kWh as heat as your boiler wasted 20% of it. So for the woodburner comparison and to compare like with like I've used the LHV energy figure of the loose logs before they go into your stove. I've also assumed that the efficiencies of the gas boiler and the wood boiler are similar at 80%.

I'd recommend that you add a fiddle factor for wood as it's simply not as controllable. You can turn a gas boiler on and off at will, but not so with woodburners. So let's add another 25% and call it 25,000kWh of demand in a year. If I've overestimated the fiddle factor, well so what, you'll have some fuel left at the end of the year.

How Much Room Will You Need?

LOGS Loose

Assuming a 25,000kWh requirement then, If you bought loose softwood logs with a potential 1030kWh per m^3, you'd need about $24m^3$ of loose logs for a year. And hardwood logs? At 1355kWh per m^3 you'd need just under $19m^3$ of loose logs.

LOGS Stacked

Neatly stacked in 1m lengths they'd take up much less room than loose; using my rule of thumb for softwood, 25000kWh at 1395kWh per m^3 would take up around $18m^3$. For hardwood, 25000kWh worth at 1835kWh per m^3 would take up around $14m^3$.

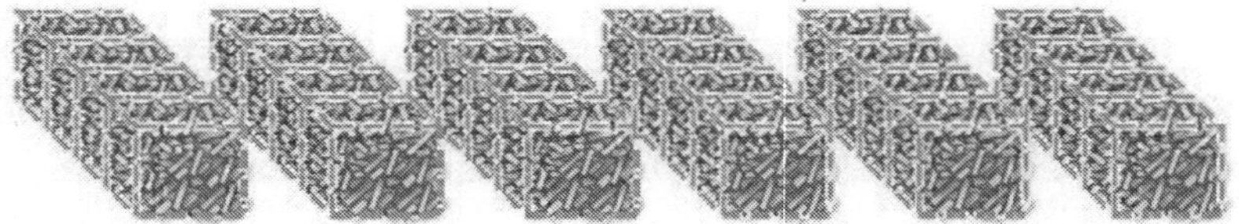

Loose logs, Softwood ; 25,000 kWh = 24 m3

Stacked logs, Softwood; 25,000 kWh = 18 m3

25000 kWh logs compared

Woodchip

First, what is woodchip? Woodchip is simply dried (to about 25-30% MC) timber comprising of trunks and branches, typically up to about 20cm in diameter and mostly from forestry sources that has been put through a chipper. This chops the wood up into small flakes about 15-100mm^2 in surface area. Unlike logs woodchip has specifications, the 'CEN TC355' specifications to be exact. These define 'standard' sizes for woodchip, which are P15, P30, P50 and P100, where P means particle size, and the 15, 30 etc. refers to the length of the chip in millimetres. As the CEN standards were based on an older Austrian 'Önorm' standard, it is still common practice to quote woodchip as 'G30', 'G50' or 'G100', where 30 is 3cm^2, 50 is 5cm^2 and 100 is 10cm^2 maximum cross-sectional area.

It's important to know the standard of the fuel that you buy as many woodchip stoves are specified to handle a certain range of sizes only and the 'wrong' fuel will simply jam the feed mechanism - for some it's a very wide range, and if buying a new stove, the wider the range the better. It is very common for woodchip systems to require woodchip meeting the 'G30' standard.

Woodchip is generally bought by the tonne, so it's easier to work out how much bulk you'll end up with. Its moisture content at 25-30% is generally a bit higher than that of fully seasoned logs. Using 25% moisture content for our example at 3800kWh per tonne - to produce 25,000kWh we would need 6.6 tonnes. Softwood woodchip is around 5m^3 per tonne at that moisture content, so 33m^3 would be needed. Hardwood woodchip would be around 4m^3 per tonne, so we would need just over 26m^3.

Wood Pellets

Wood pellets are made from very low moisture content (normally 8%) sawdust, and sometimes other biomass (such as wood chip, straw or miscanthus) that has been forced at very high pressure into a die to make a pellet. Chipped wood and other biomass must first go through a hammer mill to beat it into a mush before it can be forced through the die.

It can only reach that low level of moisture through artificial drying (heat energy) and both the hammer mill and the compression process require yet more energy. As a consequence of these costs the resultant fuel is the most expensive form of woodfuel.

The pellets look just like the 'cattle nuts' that you'd feed to cows - a poor analogy if you've never seen them either - so picture a small brown speckled cylinder about 25mm long and 6 or 10mm in diameter, with a slight glaze to it. In the case of wood pellets the glaze isn't an added glue, it's the lignin in the wood that has melted during the compression process and it acts as a natural glue for the pellet.

Wood pellets too are bought by weight, so again the sums are easy. For 25,000kWh at 8% moisture content we'd get about 4800kWh per tonne, so we'd need 5.2 tonnes. This only takes up 1.5m^3 per tonne, so less than 8m^3 would be required.

To get the difference between the types of fuel in perspective, consider the diagram here - note that the woodchip is softwood. Hardwoods take up less room.

Woodchip Softwood; 25,000 kWh = 33 m3

Wood Pellets (mixed woods); 25,000 kWh = 8 m3

25000 kWh – woodchip and wood pellets compared

What about 'Cords' of Logs?

A uniform measure used across the USA, the cord of logs, is 3.62m^3, or 4 x 4 x 8 feet long. They fall into the same category as 'stacked logs' as that's what they are, so for softwood logs at 1395kWh per m^3 for a neat stack, a cord is good for about 5050kWh. For 25,000kWh 5 cords would be needed. For hardwood logs at 1835kWh per m^3 you would get 6643kWh per cord. So for 25,000 kWh less than 4 cords would be needed.

CHAPTER THREE

'Free' Firewood

One of the venerable gardeners on 'Gardeners' Question Time' was asked 'When's the best time to get cuttings?' The answer - 'When you can get them for free'. It's the same with firewood. The very best sort is the free sort, with a few caveats as you'll see.

I'll split this chapter into two main sections, looking at scrap wood first, then grow-your-own, which is of course not really free - hence the inverted commas.

Let's look at my favourite free source then - first I must explain that I have a thing about waste - I can't bear to see it happening. When I saw the builders at a local building site lighting bonfires every day, I could stand it no longer, so I went down to remonstrate. Well, not really, I went to see if they'd give it to me rather than burn it themselves.

Scrap Wood

To get such wood for free needs a delicate approach. Look at it from the site foreman's point of view - loads of scrap pallets and sawn timber to clear up and dispose of, and that's just extra work. It costs good money to get skips on site to dump the stuff, and fires on site always cause friction with the neighbours.

You, on the other hand, may be just one of the would-be recipients circling round. There may be competitors with wheelbarrows, or those who want the odd load - they are no use to the foreman, just nuisances. So you have to look the part, enough to reassure the grizzled foreman that you'll be a benefit to the site, not a pain in the a*** (or a** if you're American). If you look like a taxman, or worse still, a health and safety inspector, he'll hate you on sight, so no suits then. If you turn up in a shiny monster four-wheel-drive, ditto. The ideal recipient for his largesse is a local and scruffy-looking farmer who has a tractor and trailer available as this means that a) he can haul the wood away without assistance from the foreman's lads and b) he probably has enough room to store the stuff so can keep the site clear.

You may think I'm kidding, but this not only worked for me. My mate who's a 'proper' farmer has been doing this for years, clearing sites with his very big tractor and trailer. He's got it to such a fine art that a couple of joiners actually bring stuff to the farm in their own transport just to get rid of it. He runs the entire heating for two houses on it with a batch boiler (more on those in Chapter 7).

So I put on my scruffy camouflage jacket, put the dog on a length of baler-band (all farmers are expected to use baler-band) and went to find the foreman. I could point to my smallholding, which was almost next-door to the building site, and I offered to take away all the scrap wood they could produce with my tractor and trailer.

The upshot was I parted with £20 (which immediately gives the lie to my description of this as 'free'), and received a promise that I could have as much as I liked, so long as I kept the site clear of scrap wood. Oh, joy. For the next 18 months or so I made regular trips with my builder's trailer, taking whatever they wanted to get rid of. I also did a bit of tree-felling for them, but as they let me have that wood too I didn't see that as too onerous. Not free then; maybe 50p per trailer-load. Maybe I should mention the odd rabbit and box of eggs that I parted with to 'remind' the foreman to ring me too...

A trailer full of scrap wood

If you can get scrap wood, DO! In the 'science' chapter I described the carbon content of wood and how much CO_2 a tree can capture - to recap, as a tree grows 1.65 tonnes of carbon dioxide will be converted to 1 tonne of tree; if the builders burn that wood they simply release that captured

CO_2, so provided that new trees are being planted at the same rate, the builders are merely being 'carbon neutral'. I'm certain they think of this all the time. However, If you can get hold of the scrap wood, it's actually better than carbon neutral as there's a net gain. Here's how the sums would work to prove it:

The builders take their scrap wood in the form of pallets, offcuts, shuttering timbers and so on and burn it in the open air just to get rid of it. The locals complain, so they chuck some of it in the skip instead and it goes for landfill. Landfill rots down, the wood is consumed by 'decay organisms' which release CO_2 as they respire; either way, the wood is converted back to CO_2 in the relatively near term. Lets say there was 1 tonne of wood - they've released 1.65 tonnes of CO_2 whether they burn it or use it as landfill. But how much potential energy have they wasted? Say it's low moisture content wood (it would be, as joinery timber), less than 20%. Per tonne, they're squandering about 4000kWH.

Meanwhile you are at home trying to keep warm by burning fossil fuels. Perhaps you have gas central heating and an efficient boiler. If you burn 4000kWh worth of natural gas, you'll produce about 734kg of CO_2.

Not only is the energy wasted by the builders, but you've produced nearly three quarters of a tonne of CO_2 that could have been saved if they'd given that wood to you instead!

The moral, to me at any rate, is clear. If you can get hold of scrap wood, and by 'scrap' I mean stuff that would either have been burned in the open or gone to landfill, you should do so, as you are not just carbon neutral, you positively save on carbon emissions that you'd otherwise have had to produce one way or another. If you were relying on fuels that gave off even more CO_2 than natural gas, say propane, you'd be saving even more - 920kg of CO_2 according to the conversion tables. Burn scrap wood and save the world. And money.

Snags with Scrap Wood.

There's always a snag; actually with scrap wood there are several.

- It can be treated with stuff you'd rather not burn; for instance old tanalised wood contains arsenic, which is given off in the flue gases. Look for flocks of birds falling out of the sky as they fly over your house. Worse, if the flue leaks and you get fumes in your house... well need I go on? Best not to burn old tanalised wood. The newer versions of tanalising fluid are much less dangerous - no arsenic. The upside is that much of the tanalised stuff can be re-used to make stuff rather than be burned, as it lasts (almost) forever.

- Nails and screws are a real hazard when you try to saw it up.

- Pallets are a pain. There's a lot of effort required for not a lot of wood. I made a 'pallet breaker' to deal with them in volume. My farmer pal's batch boiler is cavernous enough to take pallets whole, and that's the best option, but for the domestic stove they have to be broken and sawn up. As you can see, my 'Acme' pallet breaker is just a couple of short lengths of hefty beam with strips of wood nailed to the bottom to support them on edge. I lay the pallet across the two beams and deal it mighty blows with the maul until it gives in. Beware - they sometimes fight back as the wood can be very springy.

Pallet breaker

Free logs from an allotment

Offer to Fell Trees for Neighbours

This generally is really free - your payment for cutting down a tree (or pruning one) is that you take away the logs. Once you are set up to handle wood safely (see Chapter 4) then the world, as someone once said, is your lobster. Beware slight snagetts such as liability insurance. The friend or neighbour may seem quite happy to see you arrive with chainsaw and trailer, but their manner may become strained when you fell a large tree across their greenhouse/conservatory/house (delete as appropriate). I do small jobs for our Parish Council, in fact here is one such, but I keep well away from anything that looks fragile. It's up to you to assess the risks.

Grow your own 1 - Creating a Woodland

Two approaches to growing your own - a nice bio-diverse woodland with some coppicing and pollarding, or an intensive 'short rotation coppice'. We'll deal with the nice one first.

Planting a Wood

Assuming you have a bit of land, and of course, not everyone has, which bit do you plant on? There are all sorts of considerations, such as do you want to sacrifice a good grazing field long term (and this really is long term!)? Is the field full of shallow drains? Will the trees spoil or enhance the view? When planning where to plant, you'll also have to consider how you'll protect your saplings as they are very vulnerable to damage from animals, both wild and domesticated; your plot will need secure fencing. With regard to cost, the fence may be a large proportion of the total cost as the trees themselves are really quite cheap. Say you plant two hundred 50cm saplings - that might sound a lot but the trees themselves may only cost £100. Fencing wire, the sheep fence variety, may be £40 per roll, plus posts at a couple of quid apiece, then a gate - it really mounts up, so maybe that will determine where you choose to plant. We kept the fencing costs down to some extent by planting half a field, which meant that three sides were already walled (the whole field was too big for what we had in mind!), but the fencing still cost more than twice as much as the trees, so consider the potential fencing cost when picking your site.

Beyond that I can't really advise as it depends on your circumstances. There is free advice available if you know where to look, which is landowner-specific, so start there - Natural England and DEFRA websites are a good start. We used the services of the Farming and Wildlife Advisory Group, FWAG, who appear to still exist, but charge a modest fee for their services.

If you are sitting on a couple of acres or even a few hectares of land though, you'll have an idea where you would or would not like to have trees, so really the advice boils down to species choice and planting advice. Having gone through all that, I'll pass on what I've learned.

The secret of success seems to be three-fold: Buy young healthy stock, spray weeds and grass with glyphosate and use tree shelters. And here's why, in some detail:

- Buy very young 'forestry transplants'

These have been grown especially to transplant, and they're dug up and moved by the nursery after a couple of years, which helps to develop stronger roots. If you buy them at four years old they are called '2 + 2 whips', which means they were grown from seed, then moved after two years, then grown on for another two years. At that stage they may be 90-150cm tall. Smaller still are 'seedling' trees and these are cheaper - described as '2 + 0' where they've never been moved or 1+1 where they've been transplanted after a year and grown for a year. These are anything from about 40cm to 90cm and some nurseries sell them priced according to size rather than description - thus a typical example from a catalogue - Beech trees at 25-40cm may be 45p each, 40-60cm 48p each and 60-90cm may be 52p each (all these are 2010 prices). You buy deciduous trees as 'bare-rooted', which means just that, and prices tend to be low if you buy 100 trees at a time. Compare this with buying a potted tree from your local nursery (£10? £20?) then multiplying it by a hundred!

Conifers tend to be harder to handle as bare-rooted as they are not completely 'dormant' like the leafless deciduous saplings and often come in little pots or 'cells' - it means they can be more expensive too, like for like. They're surprisingly easy to grow from seed though, so if you have a coldframe it's a very cheap option to grow your own from scratch.

There's a much better reason for buying trees at the 'transplant' stage (ie. whips or saplings) - they grow better than larger trees. Larger trees are referred to as 'standards' or 'half standards' by the nurseries, and not only do they cost at least ten times as much as transplants, but after about 5 years transplants overtake the standards. Incredible but true; buy a large tree and plant it and for years it will not grow. It will survive (it had better, it cost enough!), but it won't get any larger until it's good and ready. Transplants, conversely, fairly leap up towards the light. We bought a 2 metre tree years ago and the whips planted round it passed it in about five years and now tower over it. The only people that buy large trees are the ones who feel they need an instant result and can't wait, but they are destined for disappointment. You, on the other hand, know better.

The last batch we bought were Downy birch (*Betula pubescens*) to fill a corner of a field. We bought 25 45-60cm trees at 63p each in February 2003. The photographs show them in July 2003 and again in July 2010 to give an idea of the rate of growth even in our fairly harsh location.

Above - Downy birches July 2003
Below - Downy birches July 2010

- Spray where they're going to go with glyphosate weedkiller.

That could be done as you plant, but it's much more thorough and less risk to the saplings if you do it a week or more prior to planting. Each tree needs a weed-free area around it, so it stands in the centre of a circle about 70cm diameter that's been sprayed. The easiest way would be to put bamboo canes in where the tree is going to go, then spray your 70cm circle with glyphosate well before you intend to plant so there's no risk to the saplings. If you use my favoured shelters, you'll use two bamboo canes for each one so the canes won't go to waste! When you come to plant, the grass will have changed colour so you can see if you've missed any. The snag with that is the timing - planting is best done in the dormant season when there's no frost in the ground. In Britain that's November or March and the grass isn't growing then at all so you'd have to plan well ahead, spraying in September/October when the grass is still growing.

Let's say for a moment you didn't plan that far ahead - in that case plant in the dormant season, and spray very carefully in early spring as soon as the trees and grass start to grow. Glyphosate works by contact with growing green stuff, and is systemic - it gets into the plant and is drawn right back to the roots. If you accidentally spray a dormant tree with no leaves showing it won't kill it, but by the same token it won't kill dormant grass either, in theory. Note that I say 'in theory' because the blurb on the weedkiller container emphasises that grass must be actively growing. I've found in practice that if you spray dormant but green grass in winter, it stays green until spring, then tries to grow and promptly dies and turns brown. Very odd... but back to the plot - tree shelters are great for protecting the saplings against spray drift, so you could spray after planting, but grass growing inside the shelters is protected too, so far better to spray patches prior to planting.

Why spray at all? The Forestry Commission did some experiments on the pros and cons of different methods of growing saplings, trying no weeding at all, hand weeding and spraying with glyphosate. The sprayed trees simply grew better, a lot better. I saw the test site with my very own eyes and can confirm that it's true. Not only that, it's my own experience in what is effectively a perfectly valid if unintentional scientific experiment - my neighbour planted a hedge on one side of a farm track and we planted one on the other. I sprayed my ground weeks before planting but he didn't. With similar land and similar plants, my hedge simply grew a lot better than his, and five years later it is still doing so. Grass and weeds simply choke young saplings, competing for water and nutrients, and the first year's spraying is absolutely critical to get them off to a good start. In year two it is also a definite 'must-do' job, and of course, you now have to spray with the saplings in situ, so you'll understand why I bang on about using tree shelters. Year three? It's more of a 'good thing' than an essential task, as by now they're really - what's the best term - off the ground? Out of the woods?

- Use tree shelters.

These are plastic tubes of one sort or another. My experience was that they don't need to be very long - about 50-70cm will do. They must have soft or rounded tops or the emerging trees saw their own tops off as the wind moves them about. Ones with holes in are better than solid ones.

This pictures shows two types:

Both meet the criteria of soft or rounded tops - the ones on the right are rigid shelters which come packed one inside the other like Russian dolls, and are quite expensive. They need a wooden stake (19 x 38mm slate lath cut to size is cheapest. Don't buy proprietary stakes!), to which they are fastened with two nylon ties. The black ones on the left are flat-packed flimsy affairs, delivered in bundles of maybe 50 at a time and they each require two bamboo stakes and much smaller nylon ties.

Two types of shelter

Tree shelters give the tiny tree a 'microclimate' while it's at a tender age; they prevent rabbits from eating or ring-barking the tree, and as I've mentioned, they allow you to spray glyphosate up to the base with less risk of spraying the tree.

On our first batch of trees we used tall (about 1.3m) square section rigid shelters with square tops. They probably seemed like a good idea to the suppliers as they could be posted flat-packed. For stakes we used tanalised roofing lath cut to length and sharpened. These shelters, in retrospect, were way too long - it was years before the trees emerged and they were a bit enfeebled by being protected from the wind for so long. When they did emerge the sharp tops of the shelters acted as a cutting edge and many of the trees got their tops cut clean off! The beech trees particularly did not like the still air inside the shelters and got a horrible white mould which killed a few of them and set the others back. If you've already got these damned things in place the way round the sharp edge problem is to cut a 5cm slit down each corner and bend the top over in four pieces. To allow air into the shelters for beech saplings, cut little 'windows' about 5 x 15cm on at least two sides.

We got wiser for the second batch and used the round, shorter shelters with flared tops, like the ones in the picture. Later still when we planted a long hedge we used the flimsy-looking black ones that came with the hedging pack and found them to be - perfect! Not only are they much cheaper than the rigid types, they work better, providing the required microclimate and protection against rabbits and weedkiller, but allowing air into the likes of beech saplings.

A flat pack tree shelter

If I was to do it all again, those are the ones I'd use for everything. Not only are they about half the price of rigid shelters, and flat-packed into a tiny parcel for delivery (far cheaper haulage too!), the small bamboo stakes can be simply pushed into the ground without recourse to a hammer. Or, for that matter the purchase of a large bundle of roofing lath which all has to to be cut to size.

Here's one in close-up:

After much fruitless searching on the web I had to dig out my old paperwork to find what these are called - I got them from a firm called 'Trees Please', and they're 'Planet' square net guards made by a firm called Nortene. They seem to be recommended only for shrubs, hedges and conifers, but note the birches in the 'two types of shelter'.

- we put Planet shelters on those and they shot up like, erm, rockets. If I was trying to sell them to you I'd probably come up with a good reason to sell you the tall rigid ones as they're much more expensive.
- they protect against roaming Llamas I suppose - but for my money, the minimalist ones do the job just as well, if not better.

Tree spiral

Tree Spirals

Widely used, so I'd better mention them. These tend to be used to deter rabbits, so are often called 'rabbit spirals' or 'rabbit guards', as that's their main function. The one in the photo is sort of half rabbit spiral, half tree shelter I suppose, but as purpose-made tree shelters are designed to perform a triple function, protecting against rabbits, weedkiller spraydrift and, most essentially, providing a 'micro-climate' to boost early growth, personally I'd ALWAYS use tree shelters in preference to tree spirals.

How to Plant

When you've decided what you want mail order is perfectly good for bare-rooted trees as they come well wrapped up. Get them from a nursery that's either further north than you, or local. Softy southern nurseries may be a mistake as the saplings are used to a softer climate if they are much further south than you are (this is a personal prejudice - I have no proof!).

When the saplings arrive, if you don't instantly start to plant they'll need 'heeling in'; they really can't stand their roots drying out, so need to think they're planted. I usually stick their roots in the compost heap till I'm ready to plant (as long as it's not still 'cooking'!). Gently does it - don't either damage the very fine roots or let them ever get dry.

I've already mentioned that the best trees to get are the small 'whips' or seedling trees - these are also very easy to plant. Simply dig a sharp spade into the ground and lever the earth up a bit. Then dig a slot perpendicular to the first to form a 'T' shape. Lever it up a bit and pull the spade out. As you do, slip the sapling roots into the hole with your fingers. When the roots are covered (there's a sort of water-mark on trees at the depth they've been grown at), press the turf down very firmly all around.

If using the 'Planet' type shelter the sapling usually needs to be pushed through the shelter, roots first, before planting as the shelter is floppy and can be a problem to get over the sapling's branches. If you've used these, once the tree is heeled in firmly, stand the shelter up vertically, push a bamboo stake in either side avoiding the roots and put the tiny, fiddly nylon ties in place to fasten the shelter firmly to the stakes. I mentioned not needing a hammer, but to put the stakes in I used a short length of steel pipe with one end blocked up. I slid it over a cane and used it to either push or tap the cane into the ground if it was a bit stony.

Using the taller, solid shelters, plant the sapling then slide the shelter over the top, being careful not to bend the branches down. Use a steel bar to make a hole if the ground is stony, then tap the stake in with a lump hammer to at least 30cm depth. These shelters usually have tree ties pre-fitted at the top and bottom and they just need fastening around the stake. Some have slots to fit over the stake instead. Taller shelters need taller stakes, and more substantial ones too, otherwise when the tree emerges the wind-loading, which was already significant on a tall shelter, will be such that the post will snap and the whole thing will blow over. You'll not be surprised to learn that this sometimes snaps the tree off near the base, which

Round tree shelters

is vexing when it took maybe four or more years to reach that stage. Beware advertisements attempting to convince you to use tall shelters to protect from deer. When the trees emerge you'll still have to fence the plot! You may as well spend the money on fencing from day one and use the far cheaper 'Planet' or similar shelters instead.

Spacing

Plant at about 2.5m spacings and try to avoid straight lines, if only for aesthetic reasons (it's really difficult to do! You have to keep correcting yourself or lines appear in your planting as though there's some malevolent force making you do it). They need thinning out in later years, but exactly when is a movable feast. It depends how well they grow, of course, but probably not before about eight years after planting. The thinnings can be used for your first home-grown firewood.

Species

Again, it depends what you want and where you live (acid or alkaline soil? sheltered or exposed site?) - softwoods generally grow faster and many keep their foliage over winter which the birdies like. Hardwoods can look better from an aesthetic point of view and many can be coppiced. We planted all native deciduous for the first phase, but we were planting for biodiversity, not firewood. Even so, we could have done with more evergreens for the birds to shelter in in winter, so a mixture would have been better. With the emphasis on firewood, I'd go for a few bunches of close-planted firs and pines to use the thinned out trees for logs, but many more hardwoods for coppicing, particularly ash (*Fraxinus excelsior*). Willows and poplars may grow very fast, but the wood is not terrific firewood - notwithstanding its value in short-rotation coppicing. (see below).

Take a good look around your own area before you plant and don't just rely on what you read (apart from this fine work of course...). See what grows well and what doesn't (maybe there are no beeches, or oaks, or other common species). Birch (*Betula pendula*) is supposed to be a great 'shelter belt' or 'nurse' species, which you might expect to plant at the windward side of your site to shelter the other trees - it doesn't grow at all well on our site and I don't know why. Downy birch grows much better for us. Oak (*Quercus robur*) is very often planted, but didn't do too well on our patch. Beech (*Fagus sylvatica*), after the initial tree-shelter setback, grows pretty well, and luckily those super ash trees just love us. The Forestry Commission grow a lot of lodgepole pine (*Pinus contorta*) around here. It's a North American tree and those grow OK, but spruce (*Picea sitchensis*) we've found to be even better. On our boggy patches we were advised to plant alder (*Alnus glutinosa*) which thrived, though ash seems to cope just as well.

If you want to improve your local biodiversity, plant lots of different tree types, both conifers (larch, fir, pine - of these only three are classed as 'native', namely Scots pine (*Pinus sylvestris*), juniper (*Juniperus communis*) and yew (*Taxus baccata*)) and broadleaved. The trees I classed as 'native deciduous' above are all broadleaved - beech ash, birch, alder, sycamore (*Acer pseudoplatanus*), oak and sweet chestnut (*Castanea sativa*), to name but a few. To get them established, plant 'shelter' species such as birch (grows well in most places) and sycamore on the windward side, and some conifers in amongst them as 'nurse' trees. These latter act as shelters too, and help the trees you want to keep in the longer term to grow. Plant over several years to stop them being too uniform in size and avoid straight rows if you want the planting to look natural.

Some of you will be wondering why I classed sycamore as 'native'. Well, Britain may be an island, but it hasn't been for very long, and many species that appear on the continent would probably have been here before the last ice-age that killed them off. They just shuffle slowly backwards and forwards with the ice-ages. The naturalist Oliver Rackham describes trees such as sweet chestnut (introduced by the Romans) and sycamore (maybe appearing in the 1500s) as 'becoming wildlife' at some later date, by which I think he means popping up around the place without human intervention.

There are two schools of thought on non-native species; namely those who think they should be planted here and there to spice the place up a bit, and those who are wrong. I planted a corner with western red cedar (*Thuja plicata*) for no other reason than I like the idea that the Pacific native Americans used to use it for just about everything. Maybe I'll build a canoe with it. The birds and insects don't appear to know or care that they're an 'alien' species. Besides, if anyone disagrees with your choice, a) it's none of their business, as long as you don't plant triffids, and b) tell them you're going to burn it all anyway.

For firewood, by all means plant some of everything, but major on trees that will coppice, particularly ash. Sweet chestnut coppices well, and though the wood is more usually used for split chestnut fencing, it could certainly make a good firewood.

Coppicing

Not a difficult thing to do - chop the tree down just above ground level and simply leave the stump for a few years! The new branches that sprout from the stump grow at a great rate as the tree has a huge root system to support them. Then chop those off when they're big enough to make reasonable logs and it starts all over again. I've read that the rotation of ash coppice is between 40 and 80 years. If that's the case I might only ever take one crop, so I think I'll push my luck and make plans for a second crop just before I reach the age of 110.

If you get animal damage in your particular wood you can simply cut them higher up, in which case it's called 'pollarding'; the net result is similar but it's quite a bit more dangerous for the person with the chain saw, so unless you're really intending to undergraze the trees at this stage with sheep and need the new growth to be out of reach, I'd recommend coppicing every time. Pollarded trees, in my experience at least, seem more prone to wind damage too.

What We Planted and the Resulting Wood

Starting in February 1986 we erected a fence. Really securing the plantation has to be your first move, certainly against farm animals such as sheep and cows which will just devastate a small plantation if they get in.

Then we planted 0.4 of a hectare with trees and shrubs at a rate of 1600 per hectare with a 2.5m spacing between plants; the trees were all whips, 2 + 1 and 2 + 0, all around 40-60cm bare-rooted. All in all there were about 600 trees and maybe 100 shrubs planted amongst them for that magical biodiversity. As I mentioned above, we put those nasty square section sharp edged tree shelters on the first batch, with the associated snags. Even so, the survival rate was very high at something over 95%.

The tree species were all 'native deciduous plus sycamore' (if I'm going to get picky) in this first batch, planted in little clumps of similar species, with at least 5 of the same type in a patch. We planted sycamore, alder and birch as windbreaks and nurse species (interestingly, although alder is not the best firewood, it does grow well in boggy ground, it coppices well and it even fixes nitrogen like peas do, so acts as a soil improver!). The main species, in terms of numbers, were oak, sycamore, alder, ash and beech, with a few rowans (*Sorbus aucuparia*), sweet chestnut and Norway maples (*Acer platanoides*) in amongst them. The shrubs were dog rose (*Rosa canina*) , gean (*Prunus avium*), goat willow (*Salix caprea*) and blackthorn (*Prunus spinosa*).

We had a regime of spraying for the first three years, spraying glyphosate in a rough circle just less than a metre diameter round each tree. After that they were pretty well established, but some were so puny I sprayed again in year four - the oaks particularly seemed subject to what the Forestry Commission told me was 'grass stress', and the beech trees were fairly backward too, mainly due to lack of ventilation in the solid shelters.

We planted another 0.1 hectares after about four years, with lots more ash as they seemed to be growing best of all, but with European larch (*Larix decidua*), lime (*Tilia cordata*) and sweet chestnut mixed in. In about year five we planted the rest of the field, about 0.2 hectares, with an even more eclectic mixture of beech (we'd figured out out how to grow them by this time), ash, Scots pine, Western red cedar, European larch, sweet chestnut and a load of mixed pine and fir trees grown from seed.

At the time I measured them in 2010 they were between 20 and 24 years old. They are planted on a very windy west-facing slope in the South Yorkshire Pennines at about 1100 feet (335m) above sea level. There are charts that could give an estimate of how big they 'should' be by now, but I have no faith in such wishy-washy estimations; give me real measurements any day.

There were well over a thousand trees when originally planted. Lots have been thinned out by now, but as I said, there are still a lot. Recently I used a sampling technique - I marked out a ten by ten metre square and measured every tree in the square at 1.4 metres above the ground (conveniently, that's about eye-level). There was snow on the ground at the time, not because I'm a masochist but becauase snow makes it easy to see which trees you've already measured so you don't double-count. I then did a second square, so I got results for two ten metre squares and took an average. Now ten by ten metres gives 100 square metres and 0.7 hectares is 7000 square metres, so I multiplied my average square by 70 to get a reasonable approximation of the whole plot without measuring each one.

One square contained an average of 16 trees, with a combined weight (using the formula in Chapter 2) of 1.228 tonnes. Times that by 70 and there must be around 86 tonnes of wood in the whole plot.

It's easy to calculate how much carbon - we know that trees are about 45% carbon, so in my wood there must be 86 tonnes x 45% = 38.7 tonnes of carbon.

How much carbon dioxide have they captured to produce all that carbon? 3.67 x 38.7 tonnes, which is just over 142 tonnes of CO_2. I'll just go and polish my halo...

Woodland Species Particularly Recommended for Fuel

If I've already given Latin names, I won't do it again.

Ash must be number one. A big, big reason is that it has a naturally low moisture content, even when freshly felled, at around 35% wet basis. This is around the same as many timbers after a year's seasoning, so in the 'want it, want it now' culture, you get closer to instant gratification from ash. Also, it coppices well, and from our experience on exposed upland with acid soil, it grows extremely easily and quickly. Weird, really, as it is one of the last to come into leaf in spring and one of the first to lose its leaves in Autumn. I guess it's just really enthusiastic in a somewhat short growing season. If you remain unconvinced, here's an old poem that will surely change your mind:

Beechwood fires are bright and clear
If the logs are kept a year,
Chestnut's only good they say,
If for logs 'tis laid away.
Make a fire of Elder tree,
Death within your house will be;
But Ash new or Ash old,
Is fit for a queen with crown of gold.
Birch and fir logs burn too fast
Blaze up bright and do not last,
It is by the Irish said
Hawthorn bakes the sweetest bread.
Elm wood burns like churchyard mould,
E'en the very flames are cold
But Ash green or Ash brown
Is fit for a queen with golden crown.
Poplar gives a bitter smoke,
Fills your eyes and makes you choke,
Apple wood will scent your room
Pear wood smells like flowers in bloom
Oaken logs, if dry and old
Keep away the winter's cold
But Ash wet or Ash dry
A king shall warm his slippers by.

From SolidFuel.co.uk, and many others. Possibly Shakespeare, maybe.

Beech burns well, but we've found it slow growing - how it grows in your area will be critical. It grows in some volume around here, for instance, but it seems to grow best in the valleys and more sheltered locations.

Southern Beech (*Nothofagus* species) is an increasingly popular though non-native species as it has similar characteristics to *Fagus sylvatica,* but it grows much faster.

Oak comes highly recommended, not least by Saint John of Seymour, and the late, great John knew his stuff. It's not highly successful in my neck of the woods but it grows pretty well if fairly slowly across the UK, and it makes excellent firewood.

Sycamore - ah sycamore; I've seen it called an 'invasive species', with a recommendation to 'eradicate' it, but I don't agree. On the northern uplands sycamore was traditionally the tree to plant next to the farmhouses as it would grow in these exposed places! It's been here for hundreds of years and we're not that different from mainland Europe, so I refuse to be a 'tree snob' about them. When we planted, our advisor from the Farming and Wildlife Advisory Group (the aptly-named Ms Wood), planned in as many sycamore as ash, beech and oak, and indeed alder, on the grounds that sycamore and alder would at least grow fast and well up here and act as 'nurse' species. They did too, so that's now 30 years of personal experience putting the FWAG theory into practice. Sycamore burns perfectly well when seasoned and lasts a lot longer than softwoods. It coppices well too. And another thing - it 'turns' well, so the woodturners out there can make lovely pale cream bowls out of it.

Alder - now I've mentioned it I wouldn't plant it specifically for timber, except to encourage the other, better timber species to establish. Alder will tolerate boggy ground better than most species and at least you'd get some timber! It coppices - 'fairly well' I was going to say - but in my location it actually outpaces the coppiced ash.

Birch is good to grow in the north/at high altitude/in poor soil. A good nurse crop, it is said, but we didn't find it successful on our patch. I was asked to clear birch from round a war memorial on a nearby promontory - it had grown really fast and produced a mean pile of logs from a very exposed hill top on soil just like ours, so at least you'd get some firewood if you lived in such a place! Choose Downy birch rather than Silver birch.

Grow your own 2 - Short Rotation Forestry

Before we leave the subject of woodland and consider short rotation coppicing, I should note that there's a sort of in-between version called 'short rotation forestry' or SRF. This involves planting fast growing species such as ash, eucalyptus and southern beech in regimented lines comparatively densely, felling and coppicing on a short rotation of about 8-20 years. Ideally the trees will have reached about 10-20cm diameter at breast height (1.3m) at the time of harvest.

There's a report online that was carried out for the Forestry Commission (Google 'A Review of the Impacts of Short Rotation Forestry' February 2006) which begins with that little rhyme about ash logs!

The Report was set up to consider the impact of SRF on biodiversity, hydrology and landscape rather than to comprise a 'how to do it' guide, but it's interesting nonetheless. The conclusion seems to be (I'm paraphrasing a bit) that compared to woodland, SRF is thirstier, uglier and less bio-diverse. No great surprises there then - the trade-off though is more timber per hectare.

The ideal land for SRF is lowland, below about 200m above sea level, typically in current use for growing marginal arable crops or improved pasture (ploughed and reseeded pasture). Planting is close - as I've said we were advised to plant at 2.5m spacings with a view to thinning out as the trees matured. For SRF the spacing is 2m, or 2500 plants per hectare with no thinning. It's a crop, so sub-soiling, ploughing and the use of herbicides is the order of the day as with short rotation coppicing (see below).

Obligingly, the report lists suitable species, so I'll do likewise (with Latin names if I've not previously given them).

- Alder (black, red, Italian) (*Alnus glutinosa, A rubra, A cordata*)
- Ash
- Birch
- Poplar (cultivars)
- Sycamore

- Eucalyptus (*Eucalyptus gunnii, E gunnii x dalrympleana, E nitens*)
- Southern beech (*Nothofagus obliqua, N nervosa*)

The success of eucalyptus as a crop is somewhat variable in Britain, so experiments on suitable varieties is ongoing. It seems they grow well until we hit a bad winter (such as the 2009 one!) when it's back to the drawing board. As climate change takes a grip their range will no doubt move northwards.

Short rotation forestry must be a prime candidate for carbon-capture; we're just waiting for a botanist to point out to the 'geo-engineers' that it's easier to plant a tree than to make one from plastic end electronics.

Grow your own 3 - Short Rotation Coppice

This has been in the farming press a good deal; I don't do it myself as my land is not really suitable, but I'll cover it for completeness, as yours may be!

There are two main species - willow and poplar. These are chosen because they grow really fast, but the willows and poplars grown in this system are not the bog-standard natives such as white willow (*salix alba)* or aspen, the commonest native poplar. Rather, they are hybrids created especially for the purpose. If you are after bio-diversity and aesthetics from your woodland, don't bother reading this bit because you won't get much of either from short rotation coppicing.

Where to Grow it

It's a specialist crop designed to grow the maximum mass of wood in the shortest time. It needs to be planted with harvesting machinery in mind, so you need flat land with very good access, and be prepared to pay contractors for at least some of the work. Contractors won't bring heavy machinery in for tiny little areas (just try asking one), so it follows that you need a fair-sized piece of land to grow this stuff - I don't know the minimum, and the contractor might be your neighbour, of course, but I'd guess at around a hectare at least before it's worth your while.

Here's what DEFRA have to say (see the reference at the end of this chapter).

'As a perennial crop, SRC is likely to be in the ground for up to 30 years and can reach 7-8m in height prior to harvest. Care must be taken to avoid overhead or underground cables and other services. Its impact on the local landscape, ecology, archaeology and public access must be considered alongside the operational parameters. Careful siting of open ground can minimise immediate impacts, such as having field margins adjoining neighbours' land. Hard access must be available for all machinery involved in establishing and harvesting the crop. Gate widths should be at least 4.5m but it is recommended that if new gates have to be installed they should be up to 7.2m in width. Bridge height or weight restrictions should also be considered where necessary. Ideally areas for transferring and storing the harvested crop should be adjacent to the coppice as extra transportation of this bulky crop can reduce the environmental benefits.'

This crop uses an awful lot of water, but its inherent value is too low to be worth the cost of irrigation systems, so you really need to plant it on land that gets sufficient rainfall. Indeed, when grown in the UK it uses more water in summer than all other vegetation, so DEFRA recommend that it's only grown in areas with relatively high rainfall and reproduces a Met Office map for your consideration. The hydrological research paper (referenced at the end of this chapter) gives full details.

The Forestry Commission have a practice note on the internet, dated September 2002, called 'Establishment and Management of Short Rotation Coppice', which describes the ideal soil as *'medium textured soil which is aerated but still holds a good supply of moisture...heavier brown earths with a high clay content, and often gleyed below 40cm, are well suited to SRC. Ex-pasture sites can be productive, perhaps due to the ploughed-in turf releasing nitrogen and retaining moisture as it rots down'.*

'Planting and Growing Short Rotation Coppice, Best Practice Guidelines' is aimed at applicants for DEFRA's energy crop scheme grants, and is nice and specific on nailing down the sort of place to plant short rotation coppice - land should not slope more than 15% and for preference, no more than 7%. A maximum annual rainfall of over 600mm is ideal. A maximum elevation of 100m above sea level, unless the site is particularly sheltered, is recommended. Soil pH should be between 5.5 and 7.5 for poplar (it's easy to test soil pH with a simple test kit), or 5.5 to 7 for willow. The guidelines say it doesn't really mind the soil type though, with a range from heavy clay to sandy loam being acceptable. Planting should be in twin rows 0.75m apart with 1.5m between each row to allow standard agricultural machinery to work across the crop. Plants spaced at 0.59m along the rows will give the commercial standard planting density of 15,000 plants per hectare. They've plotted various numbers of plants per hectare against mass of material harvested for the Forestry Commission practice notes (above) and found that fewer plants per hectare gives less yield - oddly, from 5,000-10,000 plants the yield stays around 12.5 tonnes dry weight per hectare per year.

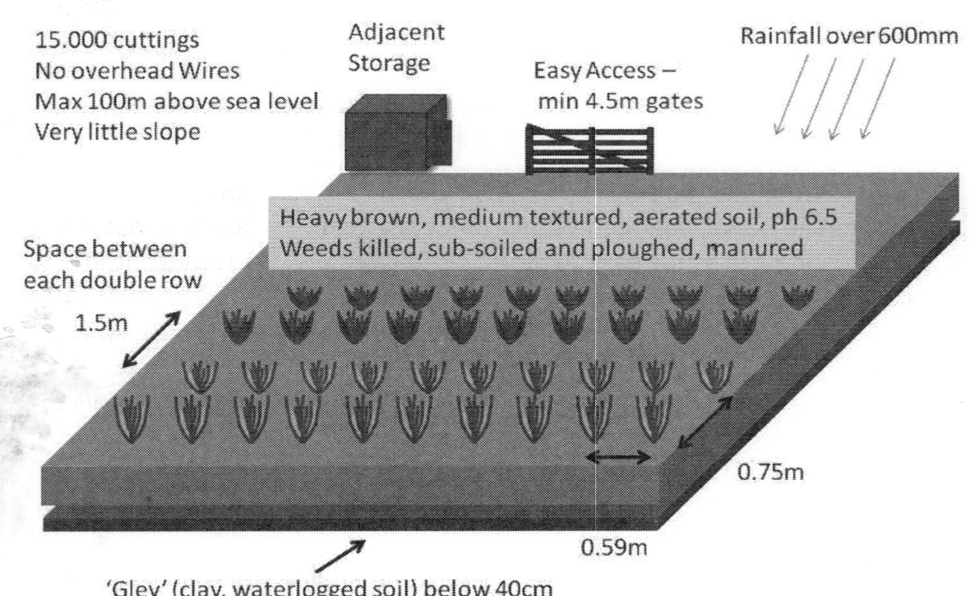

A diagram of what the perfect plantation might look like

(based on all that good advice!)

At 15,000 plants, it suddenly rises to about 17.5 tonnes. This looks to be based on a somewhat limited amount of research, but there it is, for what it's worth.

How it Grows

The stuff that's planted is actually short pieces of young willow or poplar; the ones I've been shown have been just less than 1cm in diameter and about 30cm long. The ground they're going in should be manured first - the NNCC reckons sludge or low-nitrogen manure (by which they mean well-rotted manure, definitely not hen manure), and weedkiller; our good friend glyphosate applied over the whole area, not once but twice - once in the late autumn the year before, and once before planting.

The cuttings soon start to shoot and they grow at an incredible rate - up to about 4m in the first growing season. This growth is all cut back the first winter, about February, to about 10cm to encourage the rootstock to coppice.

When harvested it can be chopped up by a modified forage harvester into 'chips' or cut into 'billets' (sticks about 10cm long); these latter are easier to store and would even be usable in a standard woodburning stove, but alas, need specialist equipment for the harvesting operation. The forage harvesting method delivers up a load of woodchip, but it's wet wood so it is not easy to store without it trying to turn itself into compost.

You get your first harvest 2-3 years after that initial cutback, harvesting between October and March, and can expect 25 to 30 OD (that's oven-dry) tonnes per hectare from the first harvest, and 30-35 OD tonnes per hectare every three years after that. We know from Chapter 2 that an oven-dry tonne of any kind of wood has an energy value of about 5300kWh; 30 tonnes would give us at least 159mWh worth of energy crop every three years, or 53mWh per year, so a perfect hectare could in theory produce enough for about two 'typical' households' heating requirements. Things are never perfect and the 'oven-dry' state is impossible to reach for all practical purposes, but a hectare should easily provide for the needs of a sizeable farmhouse.

You may wonder at this point how much energy is used to convert this type of harvested stuff to burnable material such as pellets - Woodfuel Wales reckons that it's about 2% of the material's energy content if it's dried first then processed, and 10% if it needs to be pre-dried. That's not the whole story though. Say you just convert it to woodchip to burn on your own woodchip boiler. Consider the effort required to plough, plant, apply weedkiller, harvest, chip, store etc. and all the costs involved - a short study in 'Farmer's Weekly' in 2008 valued the production costs at about 50% of the cost of bought-in chip, which is far from trivial.

Up until 2013 there is an 'Energy Crops Scheme' under the auspices of Natural England that funds about 40% of the planting and establishment costs, though I don't know what the terms are - the UK is committed to this sort of scheme though as it is a 'Renewables Obligation', so it is probably worth looking into if this is your thing. In general the resulting crop is sold on to biomass users, but that's not our concern here; we're looking at 'growing your own' with the intention of taking that right to the 'burn your own' stage, so if you do grow this stuff you need to be able to handle it and eventually burn it.

Further Reading

Short Rotation Coppice Willow (SRC) Fact Sheet, published by the NNFCC (National Non-Food Crop Centre) is a good one to start with. A mere two pages, published July 2009.

Planting and Growing Short Rotation Coppice - Best Practice Guidelines, published by DEFRA. This is much more comprehensive, and aimed at those wishing to join DEFRA's subsidised scheme. Publication date was 18th Dec 2007 so there may be a later version by now.

Short Rotation Coppice For Energy Production Hydrological Guidelines B/CR/00783/GUIDELINES/SRC URN 03/883 produced by the DTI (Dept. of Trade and Industry as was) in 2003, a comprehensive document on the water requirements of SRC. Not as dry as it sounds (ha!), it has some excellent and easy to use charts and diagrams.

Short Rotation Forestry Handbook, available on the University of Aberdeen website, but it's a 1995 document so it may be a bit outdated.

More recent stuff is the *'Short Rotation Forestry Trial in England - Overview January 2009',* available from the Forestry Commission website.

CHAPTER FOUR

Handling Woodfuels

This chapter is going to be mostly about logs as they're the woodfuel that you have to handle the most, so I'll get the easy ones out of the way first.

Wood Pellets

Of all the woodfuels these are the most highly processed form, and by far the easiest to handle. If you are used to coping with deliveries of fuel-oil for a fossil-fuel system, pellets are not a whole lot different - ideally you would have a large hopper or covered bulk store and the pellets would be 'blown' in through a pipe from a delivery truck that looks more or less like a petrol tanker. Virtually no handling at all then on your part, apart from lifting the odd lid and making tea for the delivery driver, as from the hopper the fuel gets transported to the combustion chamber in your stove or boiler by auger. The next time you see it, it's ash.

If you have no bulk storage, pellets can be delivered in tonne bags, often called 'dumpy' bags, which would be offloaded by hydraulic lifter. If the lifter couldn't get them into your under-cover store directly, you'd have to have the means to handle them yourself - maybe a small tractor with a front loader.

No tractor? The next alternative would be a pallet-load of smaller sacks then - the whole pallet is usually one tonne and the individual sacks 10, 16 or 20kg. With this method, once the truck has offloaded the whole pallet you can move the sacks individually so you don't need anything mechanical (except maybe a sack trolley).

Lastly, individual sacks can be bought, but if the delivery costs aren't going to outweigh the fuel cost you may as well collect these yourself. Even if you had that option, by far the cheapest method of getting pellets from the manufacturer to you would still be the bulk delivery, blown in method. To figure out whether it's worthwhile getting a bulk hopper, calculate your likely fuel use over say ten years (Chapter 5 shows you how), and price that amount up from your chosen supplier in bagged form versus 'blown' in bulk. Take into account that you might need fewer deliveries if you bought a large hopper.

Whichever you choose, the pellets must always be kept as dry as they were on delivery, about 8% moisture, or they will clog your stove like cement. Check the quality before you allow the delivery to be blown in though - all pellets are not of the same quality, and poor quality fuel will cause blockages just as much as excess moisture, particularly dusty fuel.

Woodchip

Woodchip is another 'bulk delivery' fuel, in this case delivered by tipper truck or 'chain-bed' truck. Both of these tip the stuff onto the ground rather than blow it up into a hopper, so your storage area will normally be at ground level or even below ground, but typically a large, well ventilated, open-fronted shed. Having said that, the odd supplier has a 'blower', but it's rare at this time.

It's the most bulky of the woodfuels by far, about four times as bulky per kWh as pellets, so it's just not economical to bag it in less than one cubic metre bags. These are the same 'dumpy' bags as before, but this stuff is so fluffy the bags will only hold about 300kg of woodchip, and of course that would be significantly more expensive than a loose load as it's been handled more by the supplier. At your end you'll really need a front-loader of some description to handle woodchip.

Kenny at Nuergy (see Further Information) proved to be an absolute mine of information on handling pellets and woodchip, and told me of the perils of letting either fuel get wet. Pellets should always be delivered very dry, at about 8% moisture, but woodchip can be very variable on delivery, and moisture content is key. Take a handful and sniff at it - if it doesn't smell like fresh pine and resin, its probably too wet! In that case, it tends to have little smell, or a stale, mouldy smell. If there is too much moisture, combustion is rather like it would be if you tried to burn a wet sheet of paper. The water would be driven off as steam, then the dried paper would ignite - well with woodchip this steam phase results in a tarry mess in the boiler and flue.

Some suppliers dry the stuff on grain floors using artificial heating supplied by - biomass! This raises the cost of production and gives me a sort of logic headache (using some of the fuel to dry the fuel to make it burn better??), but often the method is just to air dry the source wood for a year or two prior to chipping. Beware of forest chippings in mid-winter where they may have been chipped whilst frozen, and hence wet - it can be very hard to dry the stuff once it's chipped.

Size of chip can be very important. Woodchip boilers are rather touchy about long splinters which can get through the chipper. There are a couple of European CEN standards as I've mentioned in Chapter 2 which state that 80% of a sample should fall through a grid of a particular size - usually the smaller the boiler the smaller the size that it likes, so maybe 30 x 30 x 5mm for a small boiler and 50 x 50 x 5mm for a mid-range. If large stuff gets through though, it can very easily block up the feed mechanism to the boiler.

Dust can be a problem too. If there's a high sawdust content, air blasting through the combustion chamber tends to blow the dust up into the flue where it still burns, but at a low temperature, leaving tar and other residues which must be cleaned out.

An important point to note here - ALL the systems will need regular maintenance, particularly the cleaning of flues and airways; using top-quality fuels extends the periods between cleaning.

Scrap Wood

This can be used in many of the 'log' boilers and stoves, but the greatest quantity probably goes into large 'batch boilers' (described in Chapters 5 and 7). You need to be able to handle the stuff safely as it is often full of nails so is not at all chainsaw friendly. I've mentioned my Acme pallet breaker elsewhere, which is fine on a small scale, but if your main source of fuel is large numbers of scrap pallets, you really need a batch boiler to burn them on as they can go in whole. Many of the tools for sawing and chopping logs are entirely inappropriate for random scrap, due to the risk of nails, screws and metal brackets.

That said, if you are careful in dismembering pallets, they can be broken into pieces that can be chain-sawn to size for a small log-burner; also, scrap from building sites can include tons of larger timber that's been used for concrete shuttering, offcuts of wooden beams and the like that make perfectly good, if a little labour intensive, firewood.

Logs

Now we get to wood in its raw state, the log. At one end of the spectrum there's the cut, split, seasoned log delivered to your door, at which point all you'll need to do is get it under cover until you're ready to burn it. Any sort of well-ventilated shed that keeps the rain off it will do - if it's properly 'seasoned' it will be at around 20% moisture content, ie. 20% of its total weight will be water. That's so-called 'air-dry' or 'fully seasoned', as once it gets that dry it won't get any drier without artificial means as it sort of 'breathes', re-absorbing atmospheric moisture, then giving it off again to stay at around 20%. Your handling is then limited to stacking it into the boiler or stove, and of course, cleaning out the ash.

That's the expensive end of the spectrum though. The less processed the logs are, the cheaper they are, but you'll need some tools and equipment. But what equipment?

Get a Trailer!

Before a chainsaw? Yes indeed. Delivery is a significant part of the cost of woodfuel because its energy density is quite low compared to fuel-oil or coal - you can't get as many kWh into the same space! 'Buyer collects' is much cheaper, but only attractive if you have the means to take up the offer, so if you intend to burn logs, get a trailer. In my experience it pays for itself in about 3 or 4 years. Unless you are American, of course, in which case you probably already have a pickup truck.

Chainsaws

There has to be a section on chainsaws in any book about woodburning. These are the tools of the trade for the forestry men (the ones who sing the Lumberjack Song), so we need to take a look at them if we are considering handling less processed logs.

The absolute number one point to make is that these are potentially very dangerous tools. Because the blade has to be used both top and bottom, they can't be sheathed in blade guards like most power-saws, so if you intend to use one, book a training course at the same time. This book is NOT going to cover safe use of chainsaws; that's a book in itself and I'm not qualified to write it. I'll merely offer a few tips, and stress again - do a chainsaw course if you intend to use one! My own observations are as follows:

- Don't get an electric one. There's enough to worry about when cutting up timber without a blasted flex getting in the way, so get a petrol one.
- Do get a good make - my own experience has been that Stihl make really good stuff, so I can heartily recommend them. Mine's lasted 25 years so far, with a new chain every couple of years.
- Consider what you want it for and get the appropriate size. The good ones are expensive (don't expect to pay less than £200), but for cutting firewood and logs - too small (less than a 14 inch blade) and you can't cut down that big tree that's just been offered to you. Too big (over 16-18 inch blade) and they are unwieldy (so harder for us amateurs to use) and even more expensive.
- Get an electric sharpener,

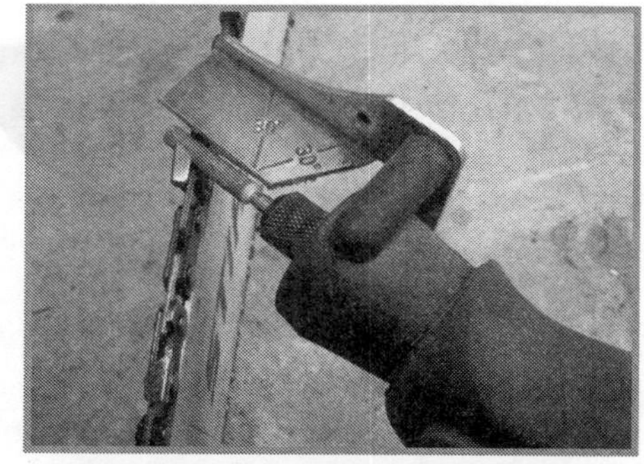

Sharpener

such as the little adapter widget that fits on a 'Dremel'-type drill. Sharpening a chainsaw blade with a file is a real pain in the fingers, takes about four times as long and doesn't get them as sharp.

- Keep it sharp! When it is cutting properly, chips of wood fly off the blade, not sawdust, and it never ever smokes. If it's sharpened properly (and that means at the right angle), it's a joy to use, so note how it cuts when the chain is brand new.

- If the teeth get beyond sharpening or you've just made a hash of it after many re-sharpenings, don't try to re-grind it, get a new chain. It's probably had enough abuse by this time and you wouldn't want it to snap.

- Don't lend it to anybody. Just don't!

- A course will have told you how to use one safely, what to wear, how to avoid 'kickback' and all that stuff, so I'm not going to even try, except to say do what you've been told as these things can be absolute buggers in untrained hands. You know the light sabres on Star Wars? A bit like that, but real.

Felling Trees

Felling notch

Assuming you've done your course, are kitted up with the right safety gear and know how to handle the saw without killing yourself, the secret of success is to practice on lots of small trees before tackling anything larger. First cut off all the lower branches to clear yourself a working area and tidy them right out of the way - you want no trip hazards in case you have to run off at some speed. Decide where the tree must fall, then cut a notch out on the side you want it to fall. The bottom cut should be horizontal, the top about 45 degrees, and a slice of tree should come out like a slice of melon. It depends on the size and shape of the tree, but about 50-60cm up is about right - above the point at which the base of the tree widens out for the roots. The notch needs to be about a quarter of the diameter of the tree in depth and is called the 'felling notch'. There's an alternative shape where the bottom of the notch is at 45 degrees and the top is horizontal, called the 'Humbolt notch', but I find it harder to cut accurately.

Felling cut and hinge

Go to the other side and from sightly above the bottom of the felling notch, maybe 5-10cm above, cut into the tree (this is the 'felling cut') horizontally or slightly down towards the felling notch. Don't cut right through though; when about 5-10 percent of the tree trunk is left, stop the saw and put it out of harm's way. The thin piece of tree trunk that's left uncut is called the 'hinge'. The tree will usually start to fall at this point but might need a push, and larger trees might need a wedge driving into the cut to encourage it to fall. Very large trees may need wooden wedges in the felling cut as you are cutting to stop the tree pinching the blade.

Once the tree is down it needs 'limbing', ie. its branches cutting off. The main surprise you'll find with chainsaws is the ease with which they jam - if you watch a professional you'd think they just keep cutting whatever, but that's only because you're watching someone who knows how to avoid this problem. When a tree is down, many of its branches are under immense pressure from the weight of the tree. Even the ones that are not will have a tension side and a compression side from their own weight, so when you start cutting you have to always bear this in mind or the saw will jam. It's easiest to learn on a low branch on a standing tree. Start with a cut on the compression side - obviously that's going to be on the low side due to the weight of the branch. That is called the 'relief cut', and should be maybe a quarter of the way through. Then move the saw to the top side and cut down towards the relief cut. The weight of the branch will open the cut as you get further through until the branch drops cleanly off. If you do it the other way round the cut will close on the saw and jam it.

Once you've got the hang of it, the tension side and the compression side of branches on a felled tree can be identified by studying the way the branch is drooping, and you can make the relief cuts accordingly.

All the stuff about 'kickback' and how to stand correctly is covered on chainsaw courses and I don't propose to cover it here or I'll get into the legal minefield of 'safety'.

'Bucking' a Tree Trunk

Bucking

To saw a felled trunk into shorter, transportable lengths (this is called 'bucking') think 'tension and compression' before you even start sawing. Study how the trunk is lying. Often they're so heavy you have no choice but to saw them in situ, at least until they're reduced enough to be moved. In a similar way to limbing, start from the compression side and make a relief cut, maybe a third of the way through but no further, then cut right through to the relief cut from the tension side. If the trunk is lying across a hollow, the compression side is the top; if one end is sticking out with no underlying ground supporting it, the underside is the compression side. This is the time you are most likely to touch the ground with the saw blade, which almost immediately blunts it; beware!

Seasoning Logs

Assuming you've now got lengths of trunk about a metre long, that's it for a couple of years as far as sawing is concerned - they need 'seasoning' now to get them dry enough for burning. Even if you don't tackle the earlier stages of felling, limbing and bucking, chances are you'll be able to get hold of lengths of green log at some stage in your woodburning career, so you need to know how to deal with it.

Black Forest log stacks

First take two long poles (tree trunks, of course) and lay them north - south where your stack of logs is going to go. The poles are just to keep the logs off the ground. The metre lengths go across these poles so that the cut ends face the prevailing wind, which I'm assuming is westerly. They should spend the whole summer like this to allow the wind to do its work, but in late autumn, cover the top with plastic sheet or some kind of roof to keep most of the rain and snow off. Uncover next spring and leave until late autumn again, but then chop into short lengths and split the thicker ones. Now put them indoors (or under the eaves if you happen to have a huge Black Forest barn like this) as they're ready to burn. From cutting down the tree they really need two years to season or they won't have reached 20% moisture content and you'll get a double whammy of less energy and more tars when you do eventually burn them.

Black Forest logs under eaves

Cutting Logs to Size

Let's assume you got or made 1m lengths and now wish to cut them into burnable logs. Some larger boilers will take half-metre lengths, so they just need cutting in two. Others, especially the smaller domestic stoves and boilerstoves need shorter lengths, but cut them into as long a length as will fit your boiler to minimise the effort.

Log saw

The safest way is to use a purpose-built saw like the one in the picture. Otherwise it's the chainsaw again, and for this you'll need a sawing horse. Unfortunately this is not a horse that can operate a chainsaw, but a sort of cross-shaped affair that holds the logs firmly in place to make them easier, and more to the point, safer to saw. These are simple to make - just follow the dimensions in the plan - so don't bother buying one. The manufactured ones are often metal too, and chainsaws and metal don't make a happy combination. You'll find that you saw into the

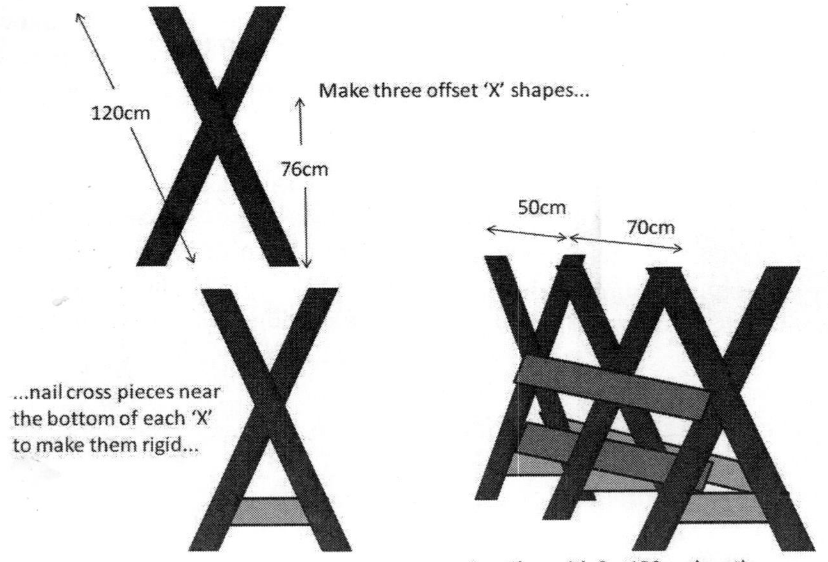

Sawing horse

sawing horse frame so often that you have to replace the cross pieces to stop it falling in half. Best to put it together with wooden dowels rather than screws too, at least the parts near where the logs will sit to keep the metal content to a minimum.

Your metre lengths simply sit in the bottom of the vee and you saw them to length - the crosses are different distances apart so that different lengths can easily be cut.

Log Splitters

Logs over about 15-20cm in diameter may need to be split before final under cover storage, as they'll burn more easily (not to mention stack more closely in the larger boilers to allow less-frequent fuelling). There are many types of splitter available, from mauls and axes to tractor driven hydraulic jobs. What you get depends on your requirements and to a large extent, your means! Personally, I've managed with just a 'Wood Grenade', sledgehammer and maul, as most of the logs I acquire are less than 15cm.

Maul and wood grenade

Manual Log Splitters

Here's a maul (a slegehammer one side of the head and a wedge the other) and a wood grenade. The wood grenade is stuck into the end grain and belted with the maul, or better still a sledgehammer, and it forces the grain apart. Effective, but it can be a little wayward, and I always use a sledgehammer rather than the maul. Swinging the maul up with the blade pointing right at my own head never seems like a great idea.

Powered Log Splitters

The small one has its own motor, but the same principle applies to both this one and the tractor mounted one - hydraulics push a wedge into the end grain and force the log apart.

Left - Petrol hydraulic splitter Right - Tractor mounted hydraulic splitter

I've seen tractor-powered splitters that look like wood-grenades but with a course screw thread (like on 'The Mole' in Thunderbirds), which rotate, powered by the power take-off (PTO) of the tractor. These purport to be faster to use than the hydraulic type. A firm called Hycrack advertises them online, complete with video. Unlike the ram type, these are used on the side of the log rather than driven into the end grain - there's a flat steel platform on which you stand the cut face of the log, then you push it onto the rotating splitter.

An aside - if you look on Youtube you'll see as many ways of splitting logs as there are of committing suicide. Don't take risks with machinery like this - if it looks like a lunatic designed it, one probably did. Buy a proprietary item.

Further Information

Nuergy (nuergy.com or ring 01506 882720) have an in-depth knowledge of all things woodchip and wood pellet, both the fuels and the boilers/stoves.

Youtube for videos of tree felling and log splitting, both for serious advice and to marvel at the fact that some of the home-made splitters haven't killed the operator before the video has ended. Especially recommended is the huge flywheel with welded-on axe head.

CHAPTER FIVE

Boilers & Stoves

In this chapter I'll take a look at how to calculate your heating requirements, then consider the various types of boiler and stove available to meet those requirements.

How to Work out Boiler Sizes

We've seen how to work out roughly how much fuel you'll need by looking back at your existing bills. But calculating the size of boiler that you'll need for a new installation is a different issue. If, as is very likely, you already have some kind of boiler, simply see what size it is. Does it meet your needs? You may think it's about the right size then. My gas boiler is rated at 16kW, and the house is warm enough, so 16kW would be my woodburning boiler size, at first sight. However, for wood we need to be more accurate than this as you'll see.

Working it out from Scratch.

There is a 'rule of thumb' on many websites that I think is plain wrong (I can't get it to work for my house, at any rate), and it's this - 'calculate your house volume in cubic metres and divide by 34 to give the required boiler size in kW'. Maybe it works in a fully insulated, draught free house, but using my house as an example - it's 285m^3. Divide that by 34 and I'd need an 8.4kW boiler. That's nonsense; we'd freeze to death. My current boiler is 16kW, supplemented by two woodburning stoves. So, methinks a little more specific detail is called for.

Using a couple of calculators on the web (just Google 'central heating calculator'), I get answers of 15.8kW and 16.6kW, which is much more like the real requirement - not only do these estimates bracket my actual current boiler size, but it's theoretically the right size taking into account all the losses, window sizes, state of insulation etc. It might not have been - with a gas boiler I could have been running it at half power for many years without really noticing, as it would simply switch itself off on the thermostat. Gas boilers don't mind being 'turned down' a bit either, they still run close to optimum efficiency.

Now you'd think that oversizing a wood boiler would be a prudent policy, but as most of the sellers seem to agree, it's not. Wood boilers run at their most efficient when they are running near the maximum output, so the recommendation is to get the theoretical 'right size' as calculated, then supplement it in times of great cold, preferably, as you're reading this book in the first place, by means of a woodburning stove.

Having said that, some boilers are described as being able to run at anything from 20 to 100% of rated output and still run efficiently, which has to be a great advantage - with many, if they are run well below maximum output tar and other deposits build up very rapidly. Most though, can't be 'turned down' to less than about 30% of their rated maximum and are really only happy running at a much higher rate.

To work around this inflexibility, an 'accumulator' is often fitted - this is a large water tank - and the stove is run at its 'preferred' output power all the time. This water tank acts as a great big heat store, and the house radiators are piped from the accumulator, not the boiler. The accumulator size is around 100 litres per kW for log boilers and 25 litres per kW for pellet and woodchip boilers. Smaller 'heat store' water tanks are often fitted along with gas boilers and perform a similar function, smoothing out the supply of heat so that you always have loads of hot water to both taps and radiators, with the boiler just 'topping up' the heat store from time to time.

Before we look at the online calculators, let's look at 'typical' requirements to act as a check and make sure you don't end up with a figure that's out by a mile!

- A small terraced house might need 10kW
- A large semi-detached house maybe 15-20kW
- An exposed, detached farmhouse maybe 18-25kW (or even more, depending how draughty it is)

Start by measuring the dimensions of all your rooms and passageways and enter the data into one, or better, several of the many online calculators. These ask questions (at least the good ones do!) such as size of windows, types of wall (solid, cavity, insulated cavity etc.), ceiling heights, number of external walls in each room (ie. are you in a terrace or detached?) and all these factors make quite a difference to the end figure.

The sellers' sites also say that getting a professional to work it out is the best policy, and maybe it is. Work it out yourself too though, as (maybe I've said this before) 'professionals' are of somewhat varying quality, certainly in the UK. It's not that I don't trust them - wait a minute though - yes it is!

Using the calculators, work out the requirements of the room that the stove will live in. Say it's 4m x 4.5m with a 2.4m ceiling with two solid external walls, one with windows, double glazed, 4m square. That works out at about 3.3kW for that one room. If your stove is intended to be just a backup to a wood-fired boiler, maybe 2kW would do. If it's to be the sole source of heat for that room a 4kW would be OK. It would be running at over 80% of its rated output. Indoor stoves are a bit less fussy than outdoor boilers to the extent that you can see them all the time and can meddle with them. In fact, that's half the pleasure of having one.

Boiler and Stove Types

I'll start with a fairly brief look at woodchip and wood pellet boilers and stoves, then concentrate rather more effort on the more popular log burners. Notice I'm assuming that a 'boiler', which usually heats water for a 'wet' central heating system with water-filled radiators, is a utilitarian thing, to be hidden from view in an outhouse, whilst a 'stove' (no water jacket) is assumed to be a thing of great beauty to be shown off in the living room. There is, of course, an indeterminate beast that is the indoor stove with built-in boiler; these are referred to in the literature as either 'stoves' or 'boilers', or sometimes 'boilerstoves', which I guess is closest to the mark.

I'd have liked to include statistics on the various types - such as how many of each type are out there now - but I can't find anything reliable.

In fact, the Government statistics that I can find suggest there were only 'between 50,000 and 100.000 wood heated properties in the UK' in July 2009, so there aren't a great number of any of them! The background material on the Renewable Heat Incentive (see chapter 9) called the installed base of domestic biomass boilers in 2009 'negligible'! The aim of that incentive is to stimulate the installation of them to get to about 300,000 domestic biomass boilers by 2020. What are the features of each type then?

Woodchip Boilers

As we've seen, storage is a big issue with woodchip, but the boiler itself tends to look rather like a vending machine with a small engine hanging from the side! This latter is an electric motor sitting between the main fuel hopper and the furnace part of the boiler - there are usually two augers, one bringing the fuel from the hopper, then an air tight valve/ chopper arrangement (which ensures that there's no 'blow-back' from the furnace into the fuel), then a final short auger which delivers fuel into the furnace. The storage issue means that a high proportion of woodchip boilers are commercial rather than domestic installations.

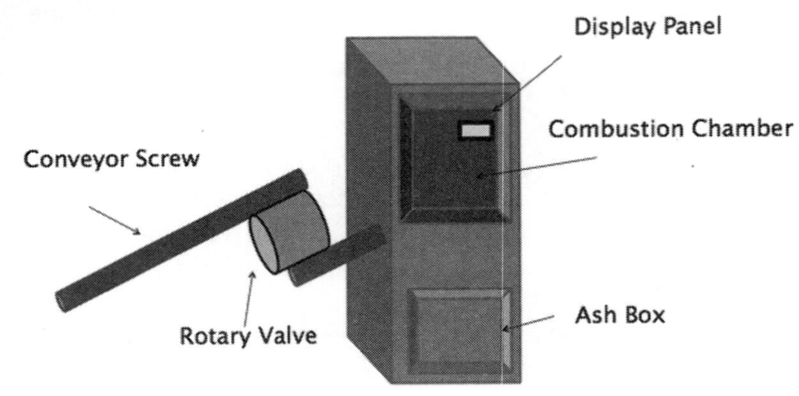

Diagram of woodchip boiler

The diagram shows a 'large domestic' sized boiler, say 15-35kW. They're physically fairly small, at maybe 1.5m tall by 1.2m deep, and 0.7m wide. They'll have air-blowing fans, either blowing air in or pulling air out of the boiler, and a 'lambda sensor' which regulates the air mixture to get the best posible combustion. They're ignited by hot air blowers.

Some will burn a number of fuel types - for example the Danish 'Refo' boilers will burn woodchip, wood pellets, grain, rape mash (obviously the last two are aimed at arable farmers), shredded timber and sawdust/shavings and the suppliers claim that it can burn most sizes of woodchip with a moisture content up to 35%.

Given the potential problems from the variable quality of woodchip and pellets (see Chapter 4), I'd certainly go for a boiler with the widest possible range of fuels, sizes and moisture content - this would also make your supply a bit more secure, in that if the seasonal price of one gets too high you can switch. You'll no doubt pay more for these more flexible boilers, but look for high efficiency too to balance against price. If you pay for your fuel, as most of us do, then over the life of the boiler about 80% of the total cost is fuel, so paying a bit more for an extra 5% efficiency is likely to be cost-effective.

The hefty looking rotary valve on the input to the boiler tends to be a feature on them all - it acts as a fire-trap between the boiler and the fuel supply to make sure the one is always separated from the other. Inside the pipes, one on either side of the rotary valve, are auger screws which pull the woodchip fuel up from the supply via the valve and into the boiler.

Wood Pellet Boilers and Stoves

Wood pellet burners are manufactured with a greater range of outputs than woodchip burners - you can buy relatively attractive stoves for inside the house as well as the larger outhouse-sited boilers. A stove designed to be installed in a living room would typically have a small fuel hopper inside the case (in fact it takes up most of the space!), holding between 10 and 30kg of pellets, which might last between 1-3 days at a medium output. Here's a cross-section through one such stove, a Calimax Solida (picture overleaf courtesy of Nuergy). There would be no auger feed from an outside hopper for this type of stove - rather it would be assumed that the pellets were stored (and probably delivered) in bags and the stove hopper filled manually.

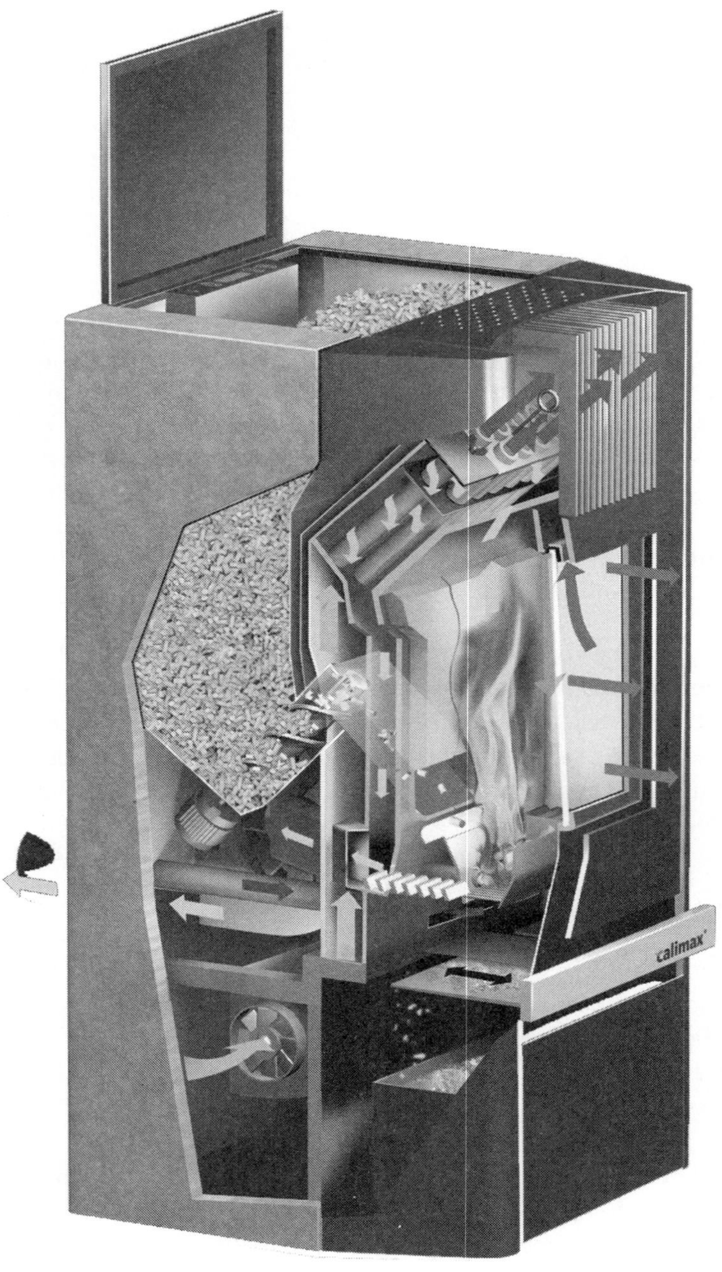

Calimax Solida cross section

A larger installation would see a well-insulated boiler in an outhouse (rather than the living room), with a large hopper outside - with maybe a 5-6 cubic metre capacity. This 'storage hopper' would have an auger or screw feed to transport the pellets into a much smaller 'fuel hopper' next to the boiler with a capacity of about one day's consumption at full power, then a further auger feed into the stove itself, so the whole thing is as automated as a gas or oil-fired boiler system. This one is a 'Janfire' pellet boiler (also courtesy of Nuergy), which is intended to fit into a utility room or even a cupboard within the house, and connect to an external pellet store of 3-4 tonnes capacity.

Janfire pellet boiler

Log and Firewood Boilers

'Batch Boilers' first. Sometimes you just want to stuff any old timber into your boiler without chopping it up or shredding it, or converting it into anything at all really. Say you have an endless supply of pallets. These are assembled using 'annular' nails (sort of jagged-looking things), which are the very devil to get out. If you chop pallets up it's a lot of effort for not much weight in wood as they are largely air - ideally you just want to shove them into some gaping maw and burn them whole. What to do? You need one of these! The pictures are courtesy of Peter Tiesen at Farm 2000 and are reproduced subject to me explaining that they're not all about shifting scrap wood - indeed there are many wood products that should never be burned such as the older tanalised stuff, so you should burn untreated wood only. Though these boilers can burn

Farm 2000 HT boilers

both wood and straw, both fuels should be dry - he specifies moisture content of 16% for straw, (so not old damp stuff then) and 20% for wood, much in line with other log boilers and stoves.

These batch-loading boilers are rated from 26 to a whopping 215kW and are really targeted at small to large farms or industrial premises. They look cavernous when opened up (you expect it to groan 'Feed me, feeed mee'!), so you do need a very healthy supply of wood to keep them satisfied. The type of scrap wood that these boilers can utilise would otherwise go into landfill, appallingly, so converting it to useful heat does the world a favour. Here's a cross-section showing what's inside one:

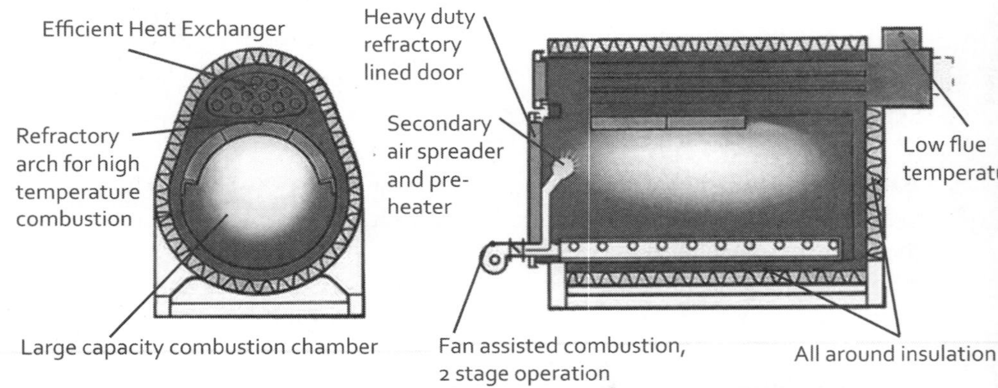

Farm 2000 boiler

Next there are very large biomass boilers on the market aimed at the likes of furniture makers and joinery shops, and no book on woodburning would be complete without a mention of them - although they are classed as 'boilers' they don't usually heat water but produce hot air, which is pumped round the workshops via ducting, and they are inevitably a good thing in terms of efficiency. Why? Because the users mostly burn timber offcuts that would normally end up in landfill, converting them into useful heat and offsetting an equivalent amount of fossil fuels. Here's one, a 'Talbott' (I believe it's a T500, 150kW) biomass boiler in our local bespoke kitchen furniture maker's workshop. Such workshops are often in smoke control areas (see Chapter 8 for what that means in more detail), so the boilers are fitted with 'afterburners' to re-ignite the output gases and smoke before it gets emitted. That's what the little box at the top of the boiler is. The fuel goes in at the right and it's designed for 'solid offcuts' according to the manufacturer - it's a pity there wasn't a person in shot to scale it, but it's over 2m high, about the same deep and maybe 1.4m wide.

Talbott hot air biomass boiler

The next size down is the 'log boiler', physically a much smaller, rather more refined affair, not at all keen on nails and large sheet material, so your wood supply has to be either logs or clean scrap timber that's been cut to size (typically 50cm lengths) before burning. This type of log-burning boiler is far more likely to be found in domestic situations than the big fellows above as these range from about 15kW up. Generally they'll be sited outside the living area, usually in an outhouse, so they are insulated in themselves and not meant to be items of great beauty. The Froling log-burner range is fairly typical, running from 15 to 60kW. Here's a working example in a National Trust site. It's an older Froling 20kW stove - it runs radiators inside the site and this one has to be loaded at least twice a day with logs that the Trust harvest for themselves from their surrounding woodland. This type of stove can be very efficient - 90% is not uncommon. They hold a stack of logs and the latest versions only need re-filling once a day - loading chambers on this type of stove are measured in litres and range from about 145 to 200 litres over the 15-60kW range. The best description is always a picture, so overleaf is what a modern Froling S4 looks like inside. Outside, they look more like fridges than boilers! Both pictures are courtesy of Econergy Ltd. This type of boiler can counter one of the

Log boiler in operation

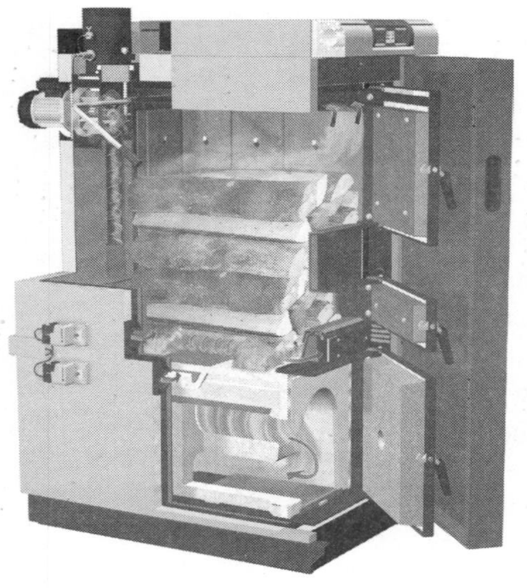

Left - Froling S4 cutaway | Right - Froling S4

drawbacks that used to be inherent with woodburning, in that they'll 'modulate', ie. burn at less than the rated output but still do so efficiently, without tarring up.

Wood Stoves (with and without Boilers!)

Lack of statistics notwithstanding, these must be the most common woodburning appliances - these are the stoves and boilers that you're most likely to see in showrooms or a neighbour's house. They are often used as space heaters only (with no water jacket to heat the domestic hot water), and very often as a supplement to other heating systems such as gas or oil-fired boilers.

They come in hundreds of different styles, from ceramic to antique to modern. The most typical in the UK, going from the showrooms and personal visits to manufacturers, is the matt black glass-fronted variety.

So let's take a look at this type of woodstove in more detail. As much of Europe and indeed the US is subject to stringent 'clean air' legislation, I'll consider a stove that can meet the UK's regulations. Chapter 8 tells you

Ceramic stove at Gibson Mill

Antique woodstove

Modern woodstove

what those are in some detail. Suffice to say here that they're intended to reduce the amount of smoke in the atmosphere. Stoves and boilers that can burn wood and meet the 'clean air' requirements are called 'exempt appliances' and appear on an 'approved list'. This being the 'United' Kingdom, there are different lists for all the regions.

Over the page is my attempt to show how one stove from the 'approved list' achieves its virtually smokeless status.

Outside air is routed from the air inlet underneath the ash tray, up inside the face of the glass in the door and enters the top of the combustion chamber. The flue at the top of the stove is the only way out, so the smoke is drawn down through the hottest part of the fire. More air is introduced to this really hot smoke so it re-ignites in the 'Afterburn Chamber', pretty well eliminating the smoke particles and adding an extra efficiency boost. Most of the water jacket area in this particular stove-cum-boiler is above the afterburn chamber, so heat is exchanged to heat the water and the flue gas is a relatively cool 285°C.

This particular stove/boiler is a Dunsley Yorkshire Multifuel Stove burning wood logs and gives off about 5kW to the room and about 10kW to the water, so would heat a pretty large living room. Typical efficiency is a claimed 75%, which is good, but not as good as some of the dedicated log boilers.

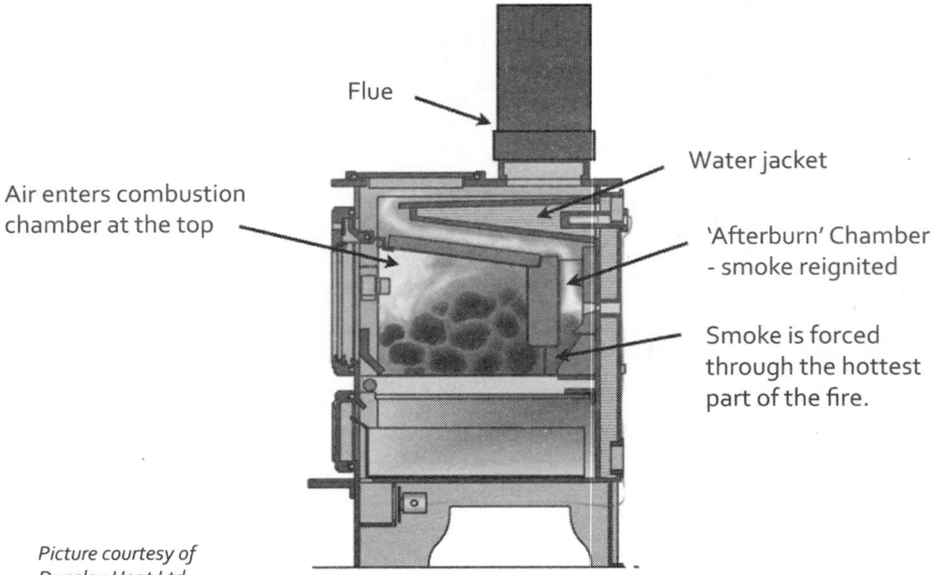

Flue

Water jacket

Air enters combustion chamber at the top

'Afterburn' Chamber - smoke reignited

Smoke is forced through the hottest part of the fire.

Picture courtesy of Dunsley Heat Ltd

Yorkshire stove cross section

Even if you're not in a smoke control area I'd recommend getting one of the stoves from the 'exempt appliances' list, just on the grounds of reducing your own personal pollution.

If funds won't stretch to that, a simple room-heating stove that works really well, burns efficiently and is simple to clean out is this one. I know this because it's my own, and it's great. My other stove is a real pain - less efficient so there is more to clean out and it uses more fuel, and worse, the firebox is wide and very narrow. This is positively hazardous as it tends to spill stuff out of the front when you open the door (which is why hearths have to be so big

Dunsley stove

- see Chapter 8, Regulations). So no picture of that one then, just the following recommendations for picking a room-heating stove:

- Efficiency should be the number one factor on your shortlist or you'll simply waste fuel.
- Get the right size for your room - use the calculators available for working out central heating boiler size and enter the room details. 2-5kW would be fairly typical for UK-sized living rooms (I know, your house might be huge, or tiny - hence the advice to use the calculator!). Oversized and you can warm up more than just the room it's in, but it might make the room way too hot if you overdo it. Damping it down makes it less efficient and prone to tarring up.
- Go for a stove from the 'exempt appliances' list if you can afford it, even if you're not in a smoke control area. Why add to the world's pollution?
- Look for a fairly deep firebox or it will always annoy you (see above).
- If you intend to burn fossil fuels as well as wood, or need the option, go for a 'multifuel' stove. Hopefully you'll be convinced of the merits of wood by now and you'll shun that option as a cop-out.
- Smaller fireboxes mean more cutting as they take smaller logs; maybe the 'right size' dictates a small stove, but just be aware of the extra effort if you cut your own logs.

Stoves with Integral Boilers ('Boilerstoves')

These look very similar to the stoves pictured above but have a water jacket and come in a range of sizes, from those which can do the job of heating the room they are in plus just the domestic hot water to heating the room + the hot water + the whole house via radiators. They come with a built-in snag though. If you want to use one of these to heat the whole house, the stove has to be running close to its peak output as I've explained above. This means the room that the stove is in gets pretty hot. Let's take this Hercules 20B model in my neighbour's living room - the spec says that when burning logs it's rated at 20kW in total, split 14.5kW (heat going into the water) and 5.5kW (output to the room). That room

Hercules boilerstove

will get pretty toasty unless it's cavernous. This is fine in mid-January but may be well over-the-top in November or April. The other snag is the refueling rate. To maintain that level of output it would need refueling every hour with 5kg of logs. You'll be kept busy.

How does my neighbour with the Hercules get round the potential snags? He uses this boilerstove in conjunction with another boiler, so they supplement each other. I'll look at how to do this in Chapter 7.

My own preference would be for an externally-sited log boiler that had to be loaded at most every 12 hours or so then left to its thermostats and fans, with a log-burning stove in every well-used living room as supplementary heat, and just because they look so lovely on a cold winter's night. If and when the equipment gets down to a sensible price, I'll install solar panels for summer water heating when the fires are all out.

Further Reading

There's a really comprehensive *'English Handbook for Wood Pellet Combustion'* online, as supplied to me by Kenny Patterson at Nuergy. Just Google the full title.

To find exempt appliances on the *Clean Air Act 'approved list',* Google 'smoke control DEFRA' or contact them on 0845 933 5577.

CHAPTER SIX

Flues

I only propose to consider domestic flues in any detail as I assume that boilers installed in outbuildings will be installed as a single job including flue, and the aesthetic considerations that would automaticaly apply to a stove or boiler inside your house will be somewhat irrelevant. If a batch boiler needs a big ugly flue, well the boiler itself is not really a thing of great beauty so you'll hardly spoil it. Not so inside the house though, where aesthetics rule, so we need to know the options.

An important and rather odd fact first - there isn't a regulation that requires us to line a pre-existing chimney. The installer is supposed to be satisfied that the chimney is suitable for the appliance and the fuel, but not lining it can lead to all sorts of trouble. In older houses the chimneys were intended for coal-burning open hearth fireplaces. They tend to be fairly big in cross-section and they've had a fairly grim life carrying foul smoke; you can't get small boys to go up them any more to clean them and replace the pointing, so many of them leak too. Not only that, the downstairs fireplace often shares a chimney with the room above, which had its fireplace 'sealed off' many years ago by persons unknown, so we've no idea as to how skillfully they did it. So use a chimney liner then.

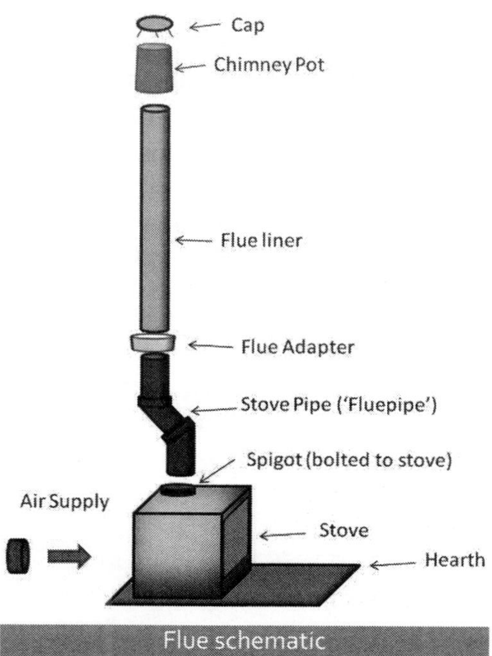

Flue schematic

The main parts of a typical

domestic flue can be seen in my diagram and the specifications for the parts are all included in the Approved Document Part J and the HETAS Guide (see Chapter 8, Regulations). In a nutshell, the stove is just one part of a system. Once you've made your choice and got a lovely stove it will not work in isolation. From the bottom and working up we have:

- ***Air Supply*** The combustion process needs oxygen, as do you. If the stove takes all the air from the room you'll suffocate and die, and of course the fire will go out (though I don't suppose that would bother you at this stage). The Regulations specify the size and location of the air inlet(s) required to ensure that this doesn't happen. Table 1 in Part J deals with the air supply and describes many options for providing a safe operating environment and this is why you need to know about these regulations - in my experience the 'professional tradesman' in all too many fields has turned out to have a limited knowledge, sufficient to do the job (hopefully), but rarely does he or she know all the options, even though they damn well should. This is your home though, not theirs, and if you want the design to be just so, the chances are there's a way of meeting your domestic requirements and staying within the Building Regulations. For each part of the installation there are many options, not just the one or two that the tradesman might be used to trotting out at every job. I know it's a sad indictment on the state of British professionalism, but that's been my experience, for what it's worth. Maybe you'll find a good one. Whilst we're on the subject of air supply, if something goes seriously wrong the risk from woodburners (aside from burning your house down) is the subtle one of carbon monoxide. It's odourless and the first symptoms are usually a headache and nausea, but it also rapidly makes you sleepy and then kills you. The detectors for this treacherous stuff used to be very expensive, but they're not too bad now, so install more than one. Certainly one in the room where the stove/boiler is sited, one in the living room (which may of course be the same room) and one in your bedroom(s).

- ***The Hearth*** The Regulations describe this as 'a base intended to safely isolate a combustion appliance from people, combustible parts of the building, fabric and soft furnishings'. Specifying 'soft furnishings' seems a bit prescriptive as the rug in front of the fire is first in the firing line, as it were, but maybe that's classed amongst the soft furnishings. There's much more detail in there of course, including dimensions, but be aware that the existing hearth may not be up to the job for the new stove. It must be fireproof and big enough so that burning embers falling out of the front of an opened stove will stay on it. Do take very careful note of this as the hearth for an existing open fireplace might not be up to the job in terms of size.

- ***The Stovepipe Part of the Flue*** The bottom part in a domestic environment is usually enameled stove-pipe, but that's still a part of the 'flue' - the regulations define this bit as the 'fluepipe'. It is just intended to connect the stove/boiler to the chimney or flue, ie. the visible bit - it should never be used in place of a flue liner. The size of it is dictated by the stove - larger stoves (over about 3kW) use 150mm diameter stovepipe, smaller stoves (up to about 3kW) tend to use 125mm diameter stovepipe. The regulations allow for a couple of bends in the flue pipe, but each should be 'not more than 45 degrees' for solid fuel appliances. See the paragraph 1.49 and Diagram 15 in Part J (2010) for the actual wording and illustrations, and be aware that this is often misinterpreted in the trade. It actually states this: *'Provisions should be made to enable flues to be swept and inspected. A way of making reasonable provision would be to limit the number of changes of direction between the combustion appliance outlet and the flue outlet to not more than four (each up to 45°), with not more than two of these being between an intended point of access for sweeping and either another point of access for sweeping or the flue outlet'.* Then we come to how the trade interprets this. My stove's instruction booklet for example states that you can only have a single 45 degree bend in the fluepipe - a literal interpretation of this would mean that the fluepipe would enter the chimney at a 45 degree slope! The accompanying diagram then shows the pipe with two 45 degree bends, which is what the Regulations actually allow. A salesman in the stove shop had a similarly weird, but equally wrong view of the Part J requirement, so read it for yourself in conjunction with the diagram or ask your 'competent person' if he or she really is

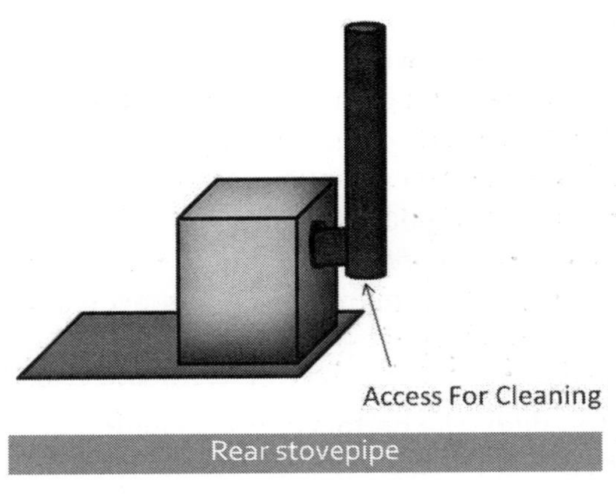

Rear stovepipe

'competent'. The HETAS Guide doesn't appear to offer a view. Anyway, from the Part J diagram 15, if the rear of the stove or boiler is used for the fluepipe connection (often this is an option, with the top opening blanked off with a plate) a 90 degree bend can't be avoided, so in this case cleaning access has to be included, as in the picture. The gist of the regulations is to both make it easy for the flue gases to escape up the flue, whilst making it easy to clean, so a flue that's as straight as possible is best. Note also that if the flue could be swept through the stove, you don't have to have an access door on the stovepipe. Some stoves can be 'swept through', some can't, so you will need to find out about your own.

The key point is that the whole length of the flue including the stovepipe must be accessible for cleaning, so if it can't be cleaned through the stove, the bottom fluepipe has to have a cleaning access door.

- ***Register Plate*** A wonderfully old-fashioned term - it's just a fire-proof panel with a hole in it for the flue that covers the bottom of the chimney hole. The stovepipe pokes through it and connects to the flue liner (let's assume it's wise to have one) out of sight inside the chimney using a specially made adapter.

- ***The Flue Liner*** As I've said, it's possible to use an existing chimney unlined and to simply poke the stovepipe through a 'register plate' and into the chimney void - if the chimney is sound you can then in theory still meet the Regulations. I really wouldn't recommend that with a woodburning stove though, from personal experience. There are all sorts of gizmos to 'improve' old chimneys and most of them are rubbish. Snake-oil salesmen will try to fob you off with various magic devices to avoid lining the chimney, such as 'spinners' to go on top of the chimney stack, or even electric fans; they'll explain that you only have problems because of the direction of the wind and the angle your house is oriented, blah, blah... Forget it. If you fit a purpose-designed flue and insulate it well, it will work (assuming the air supply to the stove is as per Regulations). What size of flue liner? As a woodburner you'll be subject to the numbers given in Table 2 of Part J - for a 'closed appliance up to 30kW' (very typical domestic stoves and boilers, that is) burning 'any fuel' (including wood, of course) the minimum diameter flue allowed is 150mm. According to table 2 though, an 'exempted' (under the Clean Air Act) stove or boiler up to 20kW burning wood could use a 125mm flue liner, but why do that? Put in a 150mm flue and adapt down to the stove size if necessary. Stoves eventually have to be replaced and you want the flue to be useable for the next one, even if it's a different size! Various options are listed in the Regulations for flue materials - a very common one for woodstoves is a double skin stainless steel flexible liner, which from experience I'd recommend. Note that it may be 'double skinned', but it's not insulated. The existing chimney pot usually has to be removed, then the liner is lowered down from the top of the chimney stack, like shoving an Anaconda into a small hole and about as tricky. They have little arrows on them showing the way up they're supposed to go because they're manufactured with an overlap which must point downwards like a funnel.

Lowering the flue into the chimney

- ***Insulation: Must it Be Insulated?*** Well it's not mandatory, but is strongly recommended. There are two good reasons for this; It prevents condensation building up, which would tend to accelerate the flue's deterioration and also, when lighting the stove the flue gases stay relatively hot as they progress up the flue, escaping from the top and drawing fresh air in at the bottom. A cold flue that cools the gases makes the smoke and fumes 'blow back' and fill your room. It's the opposite of 'hot-air rises' of course - make air cold and it sinks. As I say, this is from personal experience. A stove we had installed by 'consultants'(!) many years ago was installed without a chimney liner and it was both hell to light and often blew fumes back into the room or into an upstairs room. The chimney was both very wide and had small air gaps here and there where the pointing had fallen out, letting cold air in and smoke and fumes out depending on its whims. As soon as we fitted a proper insulated stainless steel liner - no more problems. Our neighbour would never be convinced of the need for a liner in his chimney ('they cost money'), and tried all sorts of 'cures', including spinners, cunningly shaped register plates, you name it, but still has a house full of smoke all too frequently. This is not just nasty, it can be lethal, so

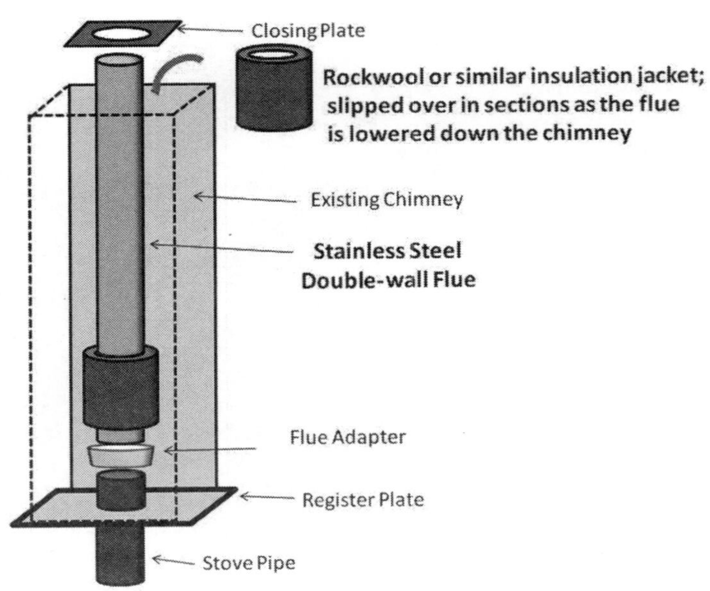

Rockwool insulated flue

don't skimp, get a proper flue fitted. Insulation can be by means of tailor-made jackets of insulation material (rockwool or an equivalent) which is put on in sections as the flue is lowered down (imagine now trying to shove an anaconda wearing a duvet jacket into a small hole). An easier option is to fit the flue in place with the appropriate brackets, fit the stovepipe with appropriate adapters, fix the register plate in place, then pour a damp mix of

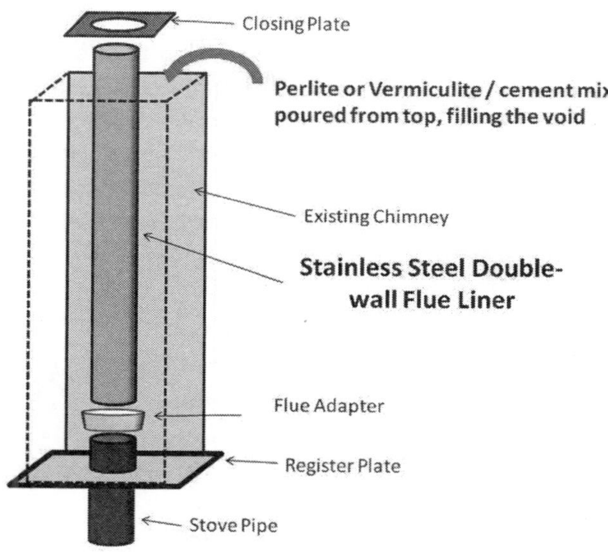

Perlite filled chimney

perlite (a volcanic glass) or vermiculite (expanded mica) mixed with cement powder down the chimney. The regulations even give the specifications for alternative mixes to use! Once this sets, the flue liner is held in place, is very well insulated and horrible old leaky chimneys become nothing more than a bad memory. The choice of the two techniques normally boils down to the size of the chimney. A really large one would take an awful lot of perlite/vermiculite and cement mix to fill the void, so it may well be much more cost-effective to use a rockwool jacket in such a case. If you do choose to use the mix, a simple way to do it is to use a cement mixer. The stuff is so light your installer may be tempted to try to mix it by hand, but its very lightness makes that really tricky; when it's dry it blows about in the lightest breeze, flows like a liquid and gets absolutely everywhere. Perlite is worse for this than vermiculite. Avoid trying to do this job on a windy day, unless you want to share the stuff with all the neighbours.

- ***The Chimney*** You're kind of stuck with its position unless you're putting in a complete new factory made chimney (see below), but Part J (2010) diagrams 17 and 18 show acceptable positions and heights. I won't redraw them here in case some engineer decides to change the Regulations, but urge you to look at the current version. The critical point is to ensure that fumes don't get back into the building, and that there's sufficient draught to make it draw properly. You may be stuck with the current chimney's position, but you may have to modify the height to meet the regulations. To give just one example, the current (2010) Part J says that for chimneys 'at or within 600mm of the ridge' (as many if not most are), the height has to be 'at least 600mm above the ridge'.

- ***Chimney Pot*** There's a particular design for woodstoves called a 'DFE' (decorative fuel effect) pot, which has a pot cover over the top to keep the rain out, like a little hat. Recommended. Having said that, there are hundreds of chimney pots - take a look at W. T. Knowles' website at www.wtknowles.co.uk. They are local to me, still have some coal-fired kilns (or had at time of writing) and have a zillion pots to choose from. It's quite an education to wander round a place like that, like a real blast from the past.

DFE pot

- ***Chimney Cowl*** If you have a suitable chimney, assuming it survived the flue-fitting process - removing and replacing one without breaking it is quite a challenge - it may still need a cowl. Many people have problems with birds nesting in chimneys; we all get rained on and rain going down the flue corrodes the stove from the inside. So either a DFE or similar chimney with a bird guard or a chimney cowl with a bird guard (I know, the cowl in the picture doesn't have one!) is recommended.

Chimney with cowl

- ***Adapters and Clamps***
These are purpose-made, usually of stainless steel so quite expensive, and it's worth knowing what should be installed just in case your 'competent person' is anything like as feckless and penny-pinching as our 'consultants' were. We've got to the top so we'll work back down again: the top plate is just a stainless steel plate with a hole in the middle to allow the chimney pot to be rebedded on the chimney masonry without stuff falling down the chimney. There's a top clamp at the top of the flue liner that clamps round the flue then rests on the masonry at the top of the chimney stack; it holds the weight of the flue, which dangles from it, so it's a vital component. Assuming you insulate the chimney, the perlite / vermiculite + cement insulation option eventually sets solid in the chimney, albeit in a crumbly sort of way, so the flue is held nicely in place once it has set: it doesn't just dangle there. The rockwool insulation option just adds weight to the flue liner, so the top clamp takes all the weight. In that respect I'd say the perlite/vermiculite option is better, but if you do go for the jacket option remember that weight and make sure your chimney top is sound! The next fitting is an adapter at the bottom of the flue liner. The flue liner has to be attached to the flue pipe, and it depends on the sizes and type of each, so the correct adapter must be used. Commonly you'd

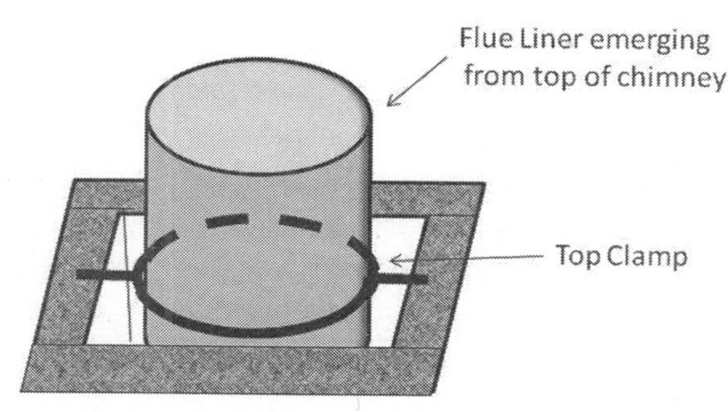

Diagram of a top clamp

be using a 150mm flue liner to 150mm flue pipe adapter. If you've got a small stove with a 125mm spigot and you're using the 150mm flue liner as recommended, then you'll be connecting to 125mm flue pipe so the adapter will also be a reducer - as is the one shown in the picture. The wider part of any socket must face upwards in a flue system as tars and sometimes condensation form inside and this runs down. The socket acts as a funnel and keeps it all inside. The joints must all be gas-tight, usually achieved by means of sealing rope and/or fire cement. Also at the bottom of the flexible flue liner and shown in the same picture is a bottom support bracket, a bit like the top clamp. This clamps round the flue liner and is attached to the inside of the chimney breast to hold the flue in position at the bottom, though it's there just to position the flue and doesn't really take any weight. The stove pipe sections fit into each other without adapters (socket end UP, of course) but must be fitted with fire cement to make them gas tight. At the top, or back of the stove, there is a spigot into which the stove pipe fits. This has to be sealed with fire cement and usually glass fibre cord too. In rare cases it may be that the spigot on the stove is exactly the same size as the stove pipe (we had one like that about 25 years ago), in which case it appears that the stove pipe is meant to sit on it socket end down - it is not! There is a final adapter available for such a stove, like a very short length of stove pipe that sits inside the spigot and presents the correct size opening for the stove pipe to fit inside.

Bottom clamp and adapter

- ***Draught Stabiliser*** Not shown on the diagram - occasionally a flue has too much 'draw' rather than too little, such that even when the stove doors are firmly closed the fire roars away. If you do suffer from that, and it's probable that you won't find out before trying out the complete stove/flue/air system, a section of flue pipe can be fitted just above the stove/boiler with a flap that partially (a minimum 20% opening must remain) closes off the flue. Maybe you'd need this if you lived in a particularly high, windy spot. We live in one of those though, and haven't needed draught stabilisers on either stove.

Other Options

There's a system available called 'cast in place' (the HETAS Guide refers to this as 'cast in situ') where chaps come along and inflate a long balloon inside your old chimney, sticking out of the top and through either a

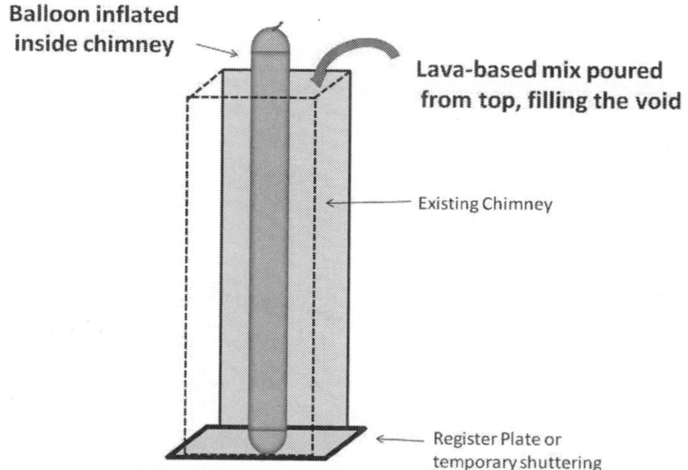

Diagram 1 - Cast in place system

register plate or temporary shuttering across the bottom of the chimney breast then, in a similar manner to the perlite option, they pour a wet mix of stuff down between chimney and balloon. The mixture in this case is described as 'a lava-based material' plus a bonding agent; not dissimilar to perlite then. Once this mixture sets, the balloon is deflated and withdrawn (can't think of a useable analogy here) and the hole

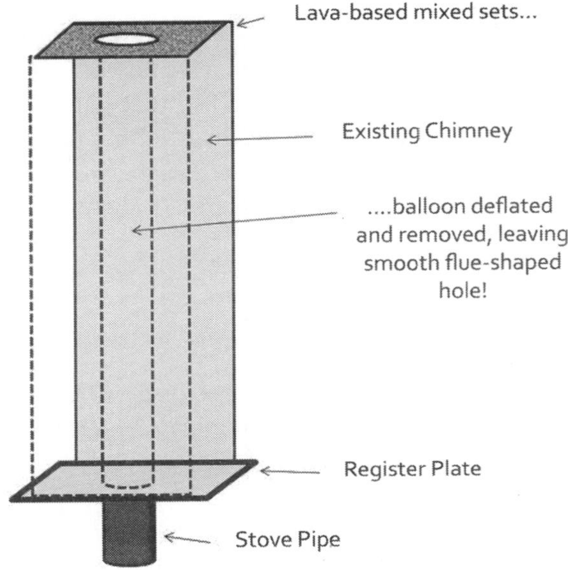

Diagram 2 - Cast in place system

becomes the new flue. I've had no personal dealings with this, but it sounds like a good engineering solution.

Another option is a sectional flue built up inside the chimney. These are called 'flueblocks', are typically clay-based and have sockets so they fit snugly together. I can't see how these would retro-fit inside an existing chimney, but maybe there's a way - they're much more likely to be used as liners in a new-build chimney. Flueblocks fit together by means of a socket at one end, which is the wider part. Again this must always face upwards so any condensation or tar forming on the inside of the flue will stay inside.

Factory made chimney

Factory made metal chimneys present a further option. Maybe you are fitting a stove/boiler in a modern house where there is no chimney or having a large boiler put in an outbuilding - the Regulations describe the specifications to which factory made metal chimneys must be made. Here's one fitted to an industrial-sized hot air woodburner (the hot air duct is to the right of the flue). This type of flue is effectively the chimney as well and is usually double skinned and insulated. Using this stuff you could site the stove or boiler anywhere (subject to those regulations, of course), so in a domestic situation you would not necessarily have to use the existing old chimney at all.

Further Reading

See the regulations and guides described in Chapter 8.

CHAPTER SEVEN

Woodburning Heating Systems

This chapter shows the more typical layouts for heating systems incorporating the various types of boiler and stove that we looked at in Chapter 5. The idea is to illustrate the wider aspects of using woodburners - what sort of storage facilities you might need for each type of system and the sort of scale we're talking about. I've put the diagrams in the same order as the boiler and stove types in Chapter 5.

In the second part of the chapter I'll consider how woodburners can be combined with existing fossil fuel systems.

1 Woodchip Boilers

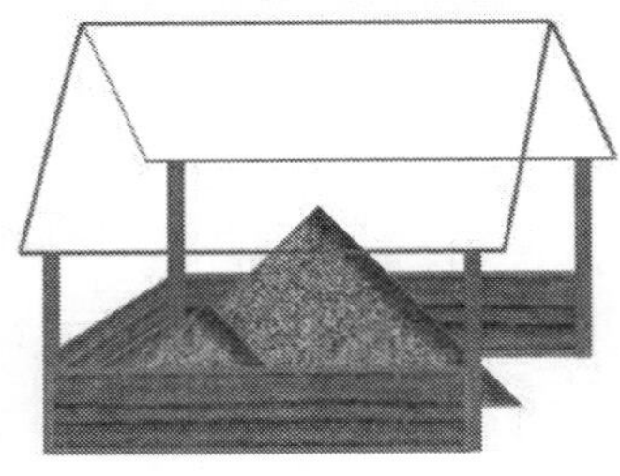

Main woodchip storage

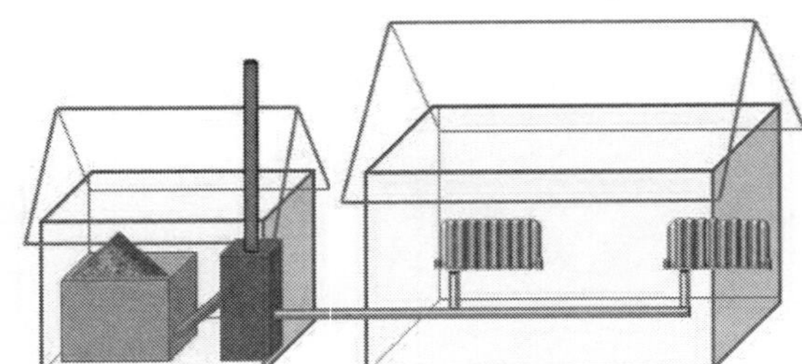

Woodchip Boiler in outbuilding, auger fed from internal hopper store

Hot water to radiators

Woodchip boiler system

As you can see, the fact that the fuel is very bulky per unit of energy means you'll need to burn a lot of it. This in turn means you need to be able to store a lot, so woodchip installations tend to be large domestic and upwards - most of them are small industrial operations, farms and community heating installations, for example. You'd normally get woodchip delivered by a large trailer or truck, so would need good access. Chapter 2 considered the energy content in some detail, and we saw that at 25% moisture content, 25,000 kWh of fuel would take up around 33 cubic metres of storage space for a whole year's worth of fuel, much more than for either logs or wood pellets. It can be 30% moisture content which would mean even more fuel, and storing a large volume of rather damp material without it turning into compost can be rather difficult, so the storage area has to be both dry and well ventilated as described in Chapter 4, 'Handling Woodfuels'.

Of course you don't have to store the whole year's worth at once - you could have multiple deliveries - but the downside is increased delivery costs and a risk of running out of fuel!

This bulk and the relatively low energy of woodchip (due to this higher moisture content), means that even the outbuilding housing the boiler will need to be correspondingly large to make room for the 'ready to use' fuel.

2 Pellet Stoves and Boilerstoves

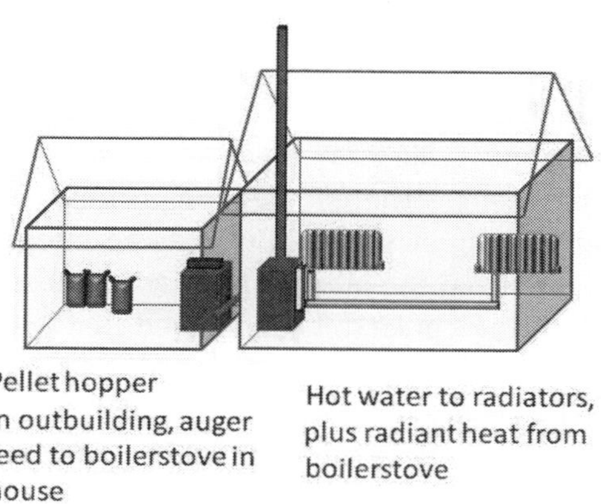

Boilerstove with pellet hopper in outbuilding

This is far more 'domestically oriented'; the most of any of the woodfuels. Pellet fuel for these stoves and boilers takes up about a third of the space of woodchip for the same energy output, so it's practical to have one of these boilerstoves inside the house with an integral hopper that can be filled maybe once a day or less. You'd still need to store fuel somewhere under cover, but a garage would do. The downside of this cosy arrangement is that the fuel is delivered bagged in small amounts, so is higher priced than bulk deliveries.

Pellet stoves are readily available as well as pellet boilerstoves - imagine the diagram without the radiators and there you have it.

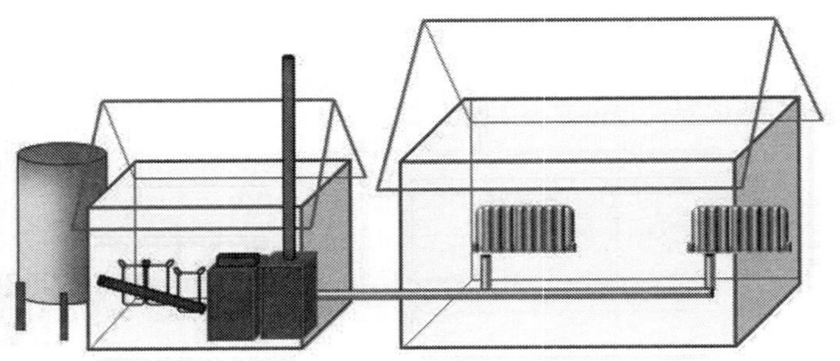

Pellet boiler in outbuilding, with integral hopper; bagged fuel or external hopper with auger feed

Hot water to radiators

Pellet boiler with external hopper

Pellet boilers on a larger scale may have an external hopper with a double-auger arrangement - there'll be one from the external bulk hopper to the internal hopper shown above as an integral part of the boiler, then a short one from the integral hopper to deliver fuel into the boiler for combustion. You could still use bagged fuel with these larger installations, but if you have the room and good access, a bulk hopper allows for bulk fuel delivery. The pellets are blown from a delivery vehicle into your hopper, so there's no manual handling, with normally a 5 tonne minimum delivery. At the other end of the scale 16kg sacks can be bought, but per tonne this might work out at twice the price of bulk (not to mention much more manual handling on your part)! In between there are pallet loads of 16kg sacks (a whole pallet at a time means less handling for the supplier), or single 1 tonne 'dumpy' bags.

3 Batch Boilers

I'm using this term to describe the large cylindrical biomass boilers such as the 'Farm 2000' type, as that's how the manufacturers describe them, though arguably other log-burners are batch-fed too. Anyway, here's the big-daddy installation showing a batch boiler with its associated accumulator tank (the bigger the better with these tanks, so it may well be even larger in physical size than the boiler). Fuel can be clean scrap wood such as pallets and timber offcuts and/or dry straw bales. Neither

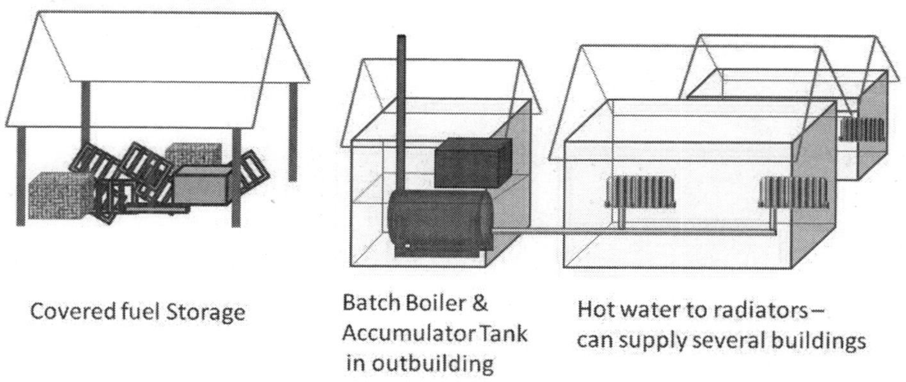

Batch boiler

straw bales nor indeed the 'miscanthus' grasses that are sometimes grown as fuel are strictly speaking 'wood', and as this book is about 'woodburning' I'll merely mention them in passing - batch boilers will burn them too, with minimal processing!

As you can see a large covered area is essential for the fuel as it can be really bulky, and batch boilers, being high output (the smallest are around 26kW, the largest around 215kW) have a voracious appetite. Very much not a domestic solution then.

4 Hot Air Biomass Boiler

Again, commercial premises only for this type. Typically found in joiners' and furniture-makers' premises; wherever the waste product is clean timber offcuts. They tend to be very large, maybe 150kW, and the output

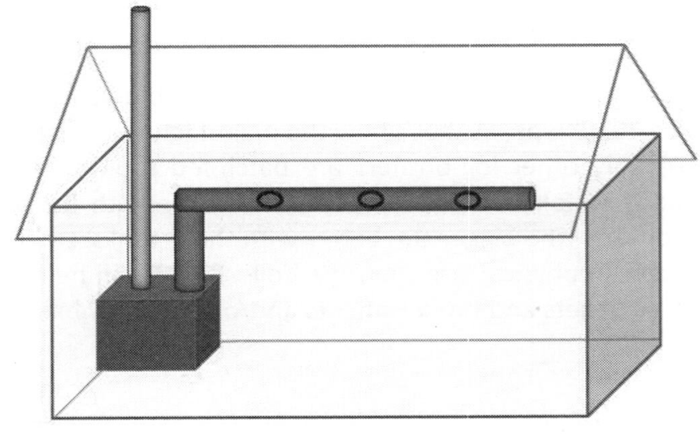

Woodburning boiler, hot air output

Woodburning hot air boiler

is not hot water but hot air which is blown round the workshop space via ducting. No wood storage is shown as it tends to be produced and stored within the heated area.

5 Log Boiler

The main fuel for these boilers is rarely scrap wood but rather logs and split logs cut to size and stacked neatly in the boiler above the combustion chamber by hand, maybe once or twice every 24 hours. The whole system would look something like this with a fair-sized covered area to

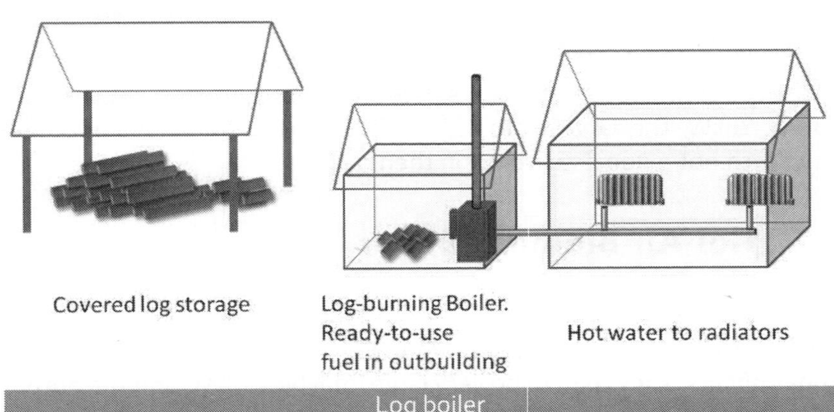

Covered log storage   Log-burning Boiler. Ready-to-use fuel in outbuilding   Hot water to radiators

Log boiler

take the logs, following at least a year stacked in the open air (covered in winter) to season - my own regime is to cut the one year seasoned logs into stove-size pieces then put them into a building for at least another 12 months. You see the external log stacks all over the Black Forest in Germany, beautiful neat rows at the side of farm tracks, the logs maybe a metre long. When they're cut and split ready to burn they're stacked under the farmhouse eaves or put in the barn.

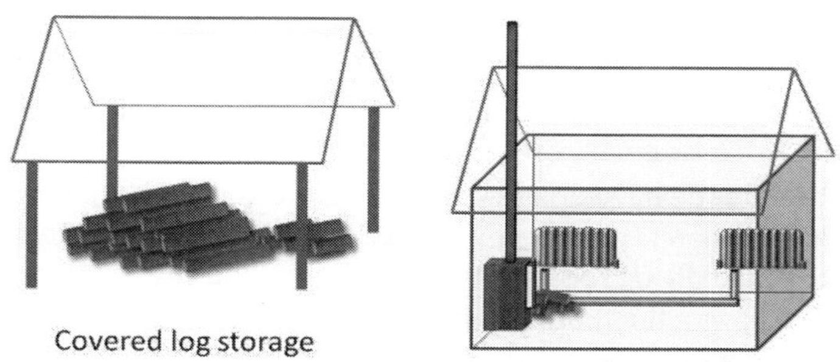

Covered log storage

Log burning boilerstove. Hot water to radiators, plus radiant heat from boilerstove

Log burning boilerstove

On a smaller scale, the log-burning boilerstove may be 15-40kW and would still need a dedicated building to store the seasoned logs as well as a piece of land to season them outside, unless of course you bought them by the small load already seasoned, in which case maybe you could sacrifice the garage or a garden shed to store them in.

6 Log Stove

The least hungry of the log-burners, the much-loved log-burning stove merely heats the room it's in; it might be 2-10kW with a smaller appetite for logs than boilers or boilerstoves, so a garage or garden shed full of logs would be more viable. As with the pellet stove, simply imagine the same diagram without the radiators and you've got the picture.

Combined Fuel Systems

If you are a purist and wish to use woodfuel and only woodfuel for your entire heating requirements, then hurrah and good for you! The diagrams above are your end point - those and a skip to dump your old fossil fuel boiler in (no, wait a minute, recycle the thing!).

Not everyone does want to ditch the old system though - some may wish to interlink with an existing fossil fuel system.

So why on earth would you want to do this? Well, for many reasons:

- You aready have an existing boiler and want to supplement it rather than replace it to reduce running costs or just to heat the main living room or the living room and the hot water.
- You have a fluctuating supply of fuel for one or other boiler type - typically you can sometimes get free wood, but it's not a guaranteed supply.
- You're a bit paranoid about your future energy supplies (like me), and want to have multiple options.
- You are now convinced about the merits of woodburning but have a perfectly sound fossil fuel system which may as well stay in situ as an emergency backup rather than be scrapped. It's just rationalising your paranoia, but why the heck not?

The simplest of all dual fuel systems would be to simply stick with your existing fossil fuel central heating/water heating system and add a stand-alone woodburning stove(s) in a downstairs living room(s). This could be either a log stove or a pellet stove as we've seen above. Thermostatic controls on the living room radiators can be turned right down or 'off', and the most energy-hungry room(s) in the house heated with wood.

This maybe sounds too simplistic, but consider the calculations for energy for your central heating requirement. Living rooms are generally calculated on an assumption of 21˚C, and tend to be the largest rooms in the house. Maybe the master bedroom is a similar size, but the assumption on the calculators is that this is heated to between 16 and 18˚C. It also has a heated room below it in most two storey houses, and

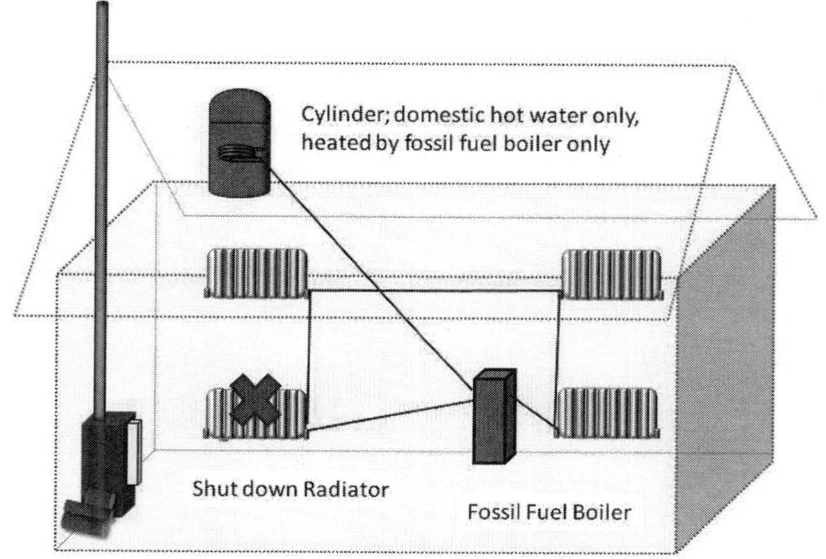

New Woodstove simply heats the room it's in.

Simplest option - new woodstove simply heats the room it's in, so radiator can be turned off.

so needs far less heat than a living room. You'd need to look at your own sums but for my house the whole house needs 15.8kW according to the calculators. The two downstairs rooms with woodburning stoves need 7.2kW, so if I turn the radiators off when the stoves are lit, I can save almost half the power from my fossil fuel central heating.

The next stage would be a 'boilerstove', an indoor stove with a fitted back boiler, and use the water heating capability to heat the domestic hot water. I've shown a log boilerstove - it could also be a pellet boilerstove.

The very simplest plumbing job would be to disconnect the fossil fuel system from the cylinder coil and connect the woodburner to the coil instead. It would be more sensible though to replace the cylinder with a 'dual-coil' hot water cylinder so that the fossil fuel boiler supplies one coil and the boilerstove supplies the other. Otherwise in summer you would need to light a fire just to get hot water and on a hot summer's day you really wouldn't want to do that. As above, leave the central heating to

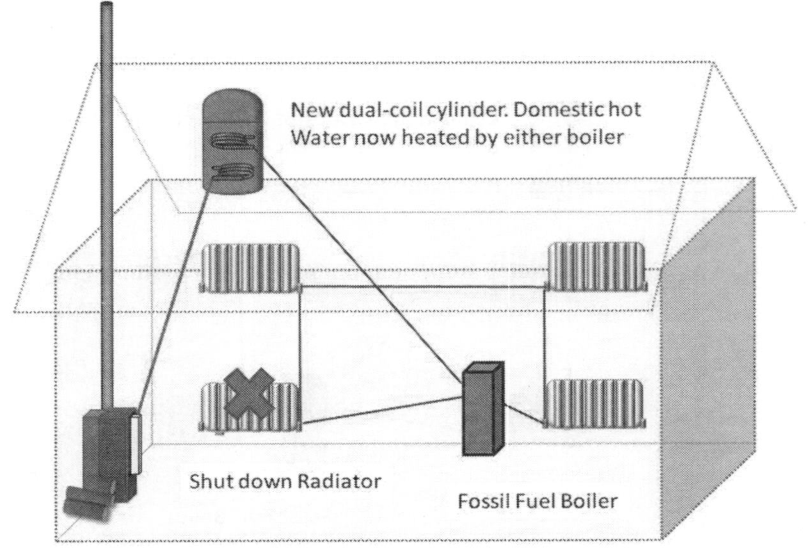

New Boiler Stove now heats room it's in plus domestic hot water.

Second option - a boilerstove fitted and used to heat the room it's in plus the domestic hot water only

the remaining rooms to the fossil fuel system. I don't believe that this can be done (without immense complexity) if your existing gas boiler is a 'combi' boiler and there's no hot water cylinder. Maybe a cunning plumber could work out how.

The next stage of sophistication, or integration, would be to install a woodburning boiler or a large boilerstove capable of taking the entire load, both hot water and radiators, and the simplest way of doing that would be to link the new boiler to the existing system by means of a passive device called a 'neutraliser'. Yet again, although I've just shown a log-burner, the wood boiler could be any of the types we've looked at, whether pellets, woodchip or even a batch boiler.

A neutraliser sounds like something Captain Kirk might have about his person, but in fact it's a fairly small, hollow cast-iron affair No electronics needed here other than simple thermostats and motorised valves, and no fooling about with the existing hot water tank.

Neutraliser C type courtesy of Dunsley Heat Ltd.

Surprisingly, as it's a passive device, one of these things can be used to link a vented woodburning boiler system (most of the woodburning systems are vented) to an unvented fossil fuel system (most of the more recent gas boiler installations are unvented, or 'pressurised' systems). There's even a layout shown in the 'Dunsley-Baker Neutraliser System Layout Options' for a combined fossil fuel boiler, woodburning boiler and solar panel which should satisfy the most alternative-supply-hungry punter - this one does call for a dual coil cylinder of course, but the solar panel is connected to one coil and the two boilers share the other.

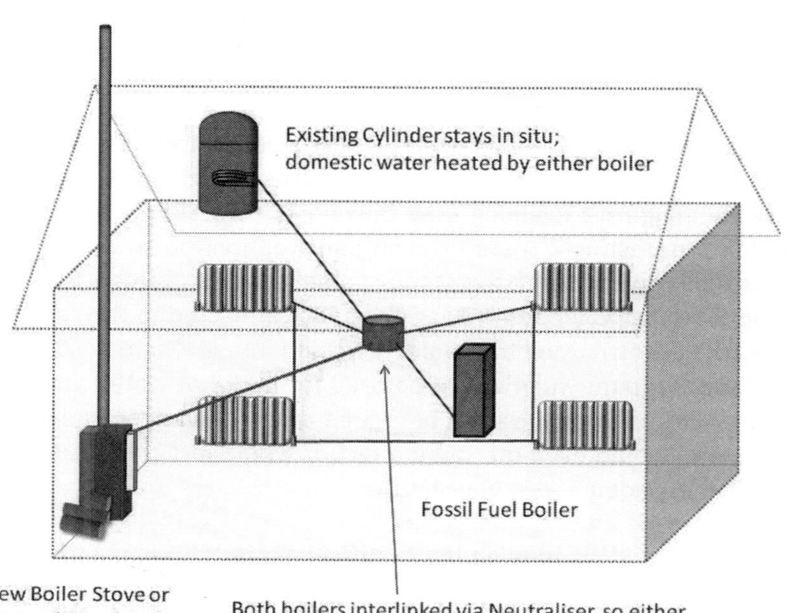

A larger boilerstove or an external woodboiler fitted, connected via a neutraliser to both domestic hot water and to the existing radiator system

There are other ways of linking them involving electronics, sensors, valves and the like, but for my money you can't beat simplicity when it comes to this type of installation, and you can't get much simpler than a hollow metal box with a few pipe connectors on it. Clever but simple engineering beats electronic complexity every time.

'Heat Stores' and Multiple Boilers

Would you be surprised if I said there were loads more options? I can't possibly draw them all out, and I've covered the most straightforward, but I must mention the use of 'heat stores' rather than hot water cylinders. They look much the same but they are usually larger than and perform a different function from a standard domestic hot water cylinder.

This is not the book to tell you all about the merits or otherwise of heat stores, it's about woodburning, but there is a chance you already have one, or feel the need for one, and if so, it's relatively easy to interlink with a woodburning boiler - the boiler is just another source of heat to warm up the heat store. My advisor from Dunsley Heat, the excellent Mr Broadbent, tells me that with regard to linking boilers to the same radiators, the heat store effectively acts like a neutraliser, so you wouldn't need both. Looking at a heat store site (Heatweb.com) I find there's a simple diagram explaining how this works - my simplified version is overleaf. Interestingly, there's a solar panel option too so you could get the best of all worlds with this set-up, namely an existing fossil fuel boiler, a woodburning boiler and a solar panel, all connected to the same heat store so all contributing to the energy going into it. The novelty here is that the solar panel heat would be used for both hot water and central heating! From a money-saving or indeed carbon-saving perspective the solar panel would have the same effect; it would just contribute to the overall energy demand in your house.

Without attempting to push the merits of these things, as I don't have any personal experience of them, the main difference from the standard copper hot water cylinder is that the whole tank is filled with water that flows through your boiler, or both your boilers if you were to connect a woodburning boiler as well, and the hot water that comes out of your taps is heated by this 'heat store' water by means of an external heat-exchanger. This use of a heat exchanger means that the water on the heat store side is completely separated from that on the taps side. The water in the heat store is always at atmospheric pressure, so it can be made from lower-spec material than a pressurised standard cylinder so should be (I don't know that they always are!) cheaper to buy, but the hot water to the taps can be at mains pressure. If you currently have a vented cylinder you can't have mains pressure hot water, but you can with a heat store.

We've come across something similar in considering the 'batch boiler' at the beginning of this chapter, which is always fitted with a large 'accumulator' water tank to smooth out fluctuations of heat coming from the actual boiler as it's stoked up and burning down. A heat store performs a very similar function.

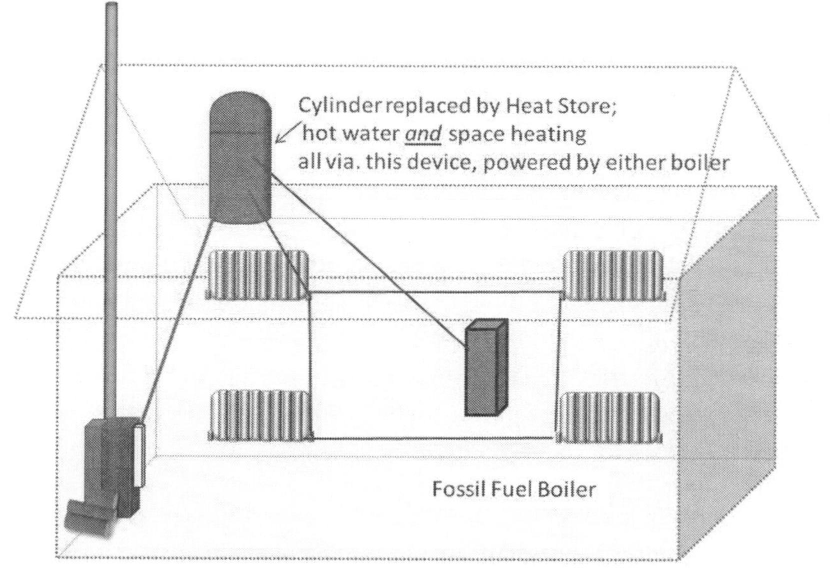

Using a heat store

Further Information

Further information on neutralisers can be found on the Dunsley Heat website (Dunsleyheat.co.uk, and look for 'linkup system'); for heat stores look on the Heatweb website (Heatweb.com, and look for 'Heatbank' thermal stores); for accumulators try Farm 2000 (Farm2000.co.uk) which has some excellent 'whole system' diagrams for batch boilers too.

CHAPTER EIGHT

Regulations

Where I give the full document names and recommend that you 'Google' them, if the given link no longer works then always choose the obvious Government website. This is normally near or at the top of the returned list and can be identified by '.gov' in its address. Otherwise you could end up with an old copy or paraphrased stuff from some random commercial site. The exception is HETAS which isn't a Government site, but 'hetas.co.uk' is nice and easy to identify!

For internet-o-phobes amongst readers, the Government documents that I refer to (all Crown copyright) can be ordered from 0207 256 7222, though the downside is that money may have to change hands. HETAS can be contacted on 0845 634 5626.

The US has its own smoke control legislation, the United States Clean Air Act, and a list of 'certified appliances' controlled by the Environmental Protection Agency. US Building Codes are set by state, local and federal Governments and would need a book in themselves, so the following applies purely to the UK.

Clean Air Act

Under the Clean Air Act 1993, local authorities may create 'smoke control areas' - if they don't the Secretary of State can step in and do it for them. If you live in a smoke control area you can't normally emit smoke from your chimney, but the Act allows for some types of stove and boiler that are particularly clean-burning to be exempt. They appear in a list of 'exempt appliances'. At the time of writing the lists for the different parts of the UK could be found here: http://smokecontrol.defra.gov.uk/appliances.php, though if that site has gone the way of all things, just put 'exempt appliances' into your search engine. The list doesn't just detail the stove or boiler though, it also states what you can burn in it!

Don't despair though, as 'untreated dry wood' comes right at the top of the fuels. To be more specific, most of the woodburners say this - *'Untreated dry wood. The fuel must not contain halogenated organic compounds or heavy metals as a result of treatment with wood preservatives or coatings.'* So there. Halocarbons deplete the ozone layer, hence the ban on burning them. This led me to look at the legality of burning MDF (medium density fibreboard) in a smoke control area. MDF is a very common wood substitute and loads of scrap is available in the UK, but it contains formaldehyde. Sure enough, DEFRA had been asked that very question, 'Can I burn MDF in a smoke control area?' - their answer, verbatim, was this - *'DEFRA guidance (under the environmental permitting regulations for England & Wales) is that the MDF manufacturing process does not use chemicals containing halogens or heavy metals so, provided clean waste wood was used to manufacture the MDF, WID does not apply to MDF combustion'.* (WID is the Waste Incineration Directive - but all Government departments can only speak in three letter abbreviations (TLAs)).

I think their answer to the question 'Can I burn MDF?' means they can't think of a reason why not, or 'Yes'. Source: http://smokecontrol.defra.gov.uk/guidance.php?a=i&q=0

Building Regulations

It's essential that you are at least aware of the Regulations surrounding stove and boiler installation, if only to make sure that you stay safe. You could rely entirely on the professionals to do a good job for you; after all, these people will always be up-to-date with the latest information, they'll know exactly what all the options are and what's best for you, and they'll always do a perfect job. Yeah, right. So how to get yourself clued up? As luck would have it, the most pertinent regulations are all available online in these modern enlightened times, but to be honest, they're a bit like wading through treacle, so I've done a precis here. It is only a precis though, so the links, or a search engine, should enable you to look up the full documents. I strongly recommend anyone thinking of a new woodburning installation to read though the three key documents.

We have to comply with Building Regulations in the UK, and to enforce that compliance there's an outfit called the Building Control Body (BCB). This is either the local authority Building Control Service or a private sector Approved Inspector (AI). Certain types of building work can be self-certificated as compliant with the Building Regulations by a member of a 'competent person' scheme without the need to notify a BCB, so we'll look at that scheme in some detail later. The main documents first:

There are three key documents (plus any number of British standards referred to by them) that we need to be aware of - these are:

- Domestic Building Services Compliance Guide
- Approved Document Part J (Combustion Appliances and Fuel Storage Systems)
- HETAS Guide references to three more documents are made in the above; these are:
- Approved Document Part L1A (Conservation of Fuel and Power in New Dwellings)
- Approved Document Part L1B (Conservation of Fuel and Power in Existing Dwellings)
- Approved Document Part F (Ventilation)

These latter three are far less relevant in that they tend to simply refer us back to the first three! Eventually we'll disappear up our own flues...

First, the Domestic Building Services Compliance Guide 2010

This is a guide to the Regulations, and the full document could be found here at the time of writing (if it's shuffled off elsewhere, Google the full title and look for the pdf file):

http://live.planningportal.gov.uk/uploads/br/domestic_building_compliance_guide_2010.pdf

Its scope is given as follows: *This guide provides detailed guidance for persons installing fixed building services in new and existing domestic buildings to help them comply with Building Regulations. It covers work on both new systems and replacement systems, identifying the differing requirements where these exist*. This edition of the guide covers conventional means of providing primary space heating, domestic hot water, mechanical ventilation - there's more, but those are the parts that concern us here.

Such guides are officially sanctioned documents that offer an interpretation of the Building Regulations, offering practical guidance to installers and builders. There is a tacit admission here that the Building Regulations are so obscure and complex that they need interpretation for builders, which I'd have thought was an admission of failure on the part of the authors, but I bet they feel no guilt. I did a year or two writing technical guides at work, and the older stuff was written in awful pseudo-legalese, as if someone other than a human, a lawyer maybe, had written it. We found that if we wrote the new stuff in plain English they were both easier to read and the guidance was much more likely to be followed. Such a revelation hasn't found its way to the Civil Service yet.

Anyway, the documents that do this 'translation into plain English' function are called Approved Documents in England and Wales, Technical Handbooks in Scotland and Technical Booklets in Northern Ireland. This Compliance Guide 2010 is an Approved Document. You'd think that following its advice would mean your installation would be strictly kosher, but not necessarily. It states: '*Note: Following guidance in an Approved Document, Technical Handbook or Technical Booklet does not guarantee compliance with Building Regulations...in every case it is for the Building Control Body to decide whether work complies with Building Regulations*'.

There is a legal presumption that if you follow its guidance, you'll comply with the Building Regulations though, so let's press on - stoves and boilers are classed as 'fixed building services' in that they provide fixed systems for heating and hot water, so are definitely within its scope.

The first point to note from the Guide is that: *When replacing an existing appliance, the efficiency of the new appliance should not be significantly less than the efficiency of the appliance being replaced. If the replacement involves a fuel switch, then the relative carbon emissions associated with the new and existing fuels should be considered when assessing the reasonableness of the proposed new appliance. The aim is to discourage replacement of an existing appliance by a significantly less carbon efficient one*'.

So if you want to replace say an oil-fired boiler with 72% efficiency with a woodburning boiler of 65%, can you do it? The guide says 'yes' - even though the new boiler is less efficient in terms of power in vs power out, it is far more carbon efficient; the Guide shows a worked example, and gives (or tells you where to obtain) all the carbon efficiency figures that you need to work out the sums.

Chapter 5 is the key chapter for woodburners, with table 18 giving minimum efficiency requirements for all types. No point trotting them all out here as this sort of guidance is subject to constant tinkering by civil servants, but in the April 2010 Guide, to take a relevant example, a woodburning stove with no back boiler burning logs only must have an efficiency of not less than 65%. So if you install one as a new or replacement system with less than that efficiency, you will be in breach of the Building Regulations, which is why you need to be aware of this stuff!

Now there are many references within this guide to an outfit called 'HETAS', and to documents that they publish. Who are they?

HETAS

The Heating Equipment Testing and Approval Scheme which is (as it says on their website) 'the independent UK body recognised by DEFRA for the official testing and approval of domestic solid fuels, solid fuel and wood burning appliances and associated equipment and services'. They're an umbrella body for much of the industry - for instance they represent the Solid Fuel Association, the National Fireplace Association and several others, including the Government body they refer to, the Department for Environment, Food and Rural Affairs (DEFRA).

HETAS Guide

HETAS publishes an Official Guide at http://www.hetas.co.uk/public/hetas_guide.html (or Google 'HETAS Guide' if it's wandered off). Now although this doesn't have the status of Building Regulations or Approved Documents, it does get referred to by the latter as a source of information and guidance. The HETAS Guide has four main parts covering 1) stoves and boilers that meet HETAS standards, and hence (if fitted correctly), the Building Regulations; 2) fuels, though much of that is about fossil fuels in which we are not interested; 3) factory made chimneys and chimney lining systems and 4) care and maintenance.

Say for example that you've looked at Chapter 6 on flues and decided that a cast-on-site concrete lining system will be just the job. The HETAS Guide part 3 Section J will tell you a bit more about how one works, and list a couple of companies that meet the HETAS specifications (and in turn, the appropriate British standards and the Building Regulations).

A book such as mine can't keep up with changing requirements and take account of companies starting up and disappearing, so it's no point my listing names and addresses - the current HETAS Guide does that for us.

Competent Persons

Now we've met HETAS, it might be a good time to introduce the 'competent person' schemes. Any installer has to comply with a whole load of regulations as we can see. How can we be sure that they do? We choose one who's registered with a 'competent person' scheme, that's how. Such a person can not only carry out the work but can self-certify it. In fact he or she must issue you with a certificate within 30 days of completing the work, confirming that it complies with all applicable Building Regulation requirements.

The alternative to self-certification would be to notify the local Council (the aforementioned Building Control Body), get the Building Inspector involved and pay the subsequent fees.

The official Government website http://www.communities.gov.uk/planningandbuilding/buildingregulations/competentpersonsschemes/ (or Google 'Competent Persons Scheme'), lists the following as authorised schemes for installers of solid fuel installations, including biomass:

APHC (but not for appliances over 100 kilowatts output or in buildings of more than three storeys), BESCA, CORGI, ELECSA, HETAS, NAPIT, NICEIC. Now I noted a recent exchange of polite abuse between CORGI and HETAS about competence and demarcation, but the existing Competent Person Scheme quite clearly includes both, and others! So for your installation, as long as your installer is registered with one of these bodies, he or she should be competent to carry out a safe and compliant job, and self-certify it. It may be that the 'competent person' will be happy to let you help with the installation to keep the costs down, but they then have to certify that it has been done to the correct standard.

I am told that there are proposals to introduce similar requirements for 'competent persons' under Scottish Building Regulations and there is a voluntary Scottish HETAS/SFA scheme for engineers operating at the moment.

Approved Document Part J Combustion Appliances and Fuel Storage Systems 1 October 2010

Heavy going but vital, and available here: http://www.planningportal.gov.uk/uploads/br/BR_PDF_ADJ_2010.pdf or Google 'Approved Document Part J'.

The main sections of Part J of interest to woodburners are:

- J0 General Guidance - this part has definitions and diagrams.
- J1 Air Supply - for example, there must be enough for combustion, to prevent overheating and for the efficient working of any flue.
- J2 Discharge of Products of Combustion - Flues! If you look at Chapter 6 Flues you'll see that a lot of the information in that chapter refers to guidance given in both sections J1 and J2.
- J2A Warning of Release of Carbon Monoxide
- J3 Protection of Buildings - this part describes how to install stoves, boilers and flues without burning the building down.
- J4 Provision of Information - attaching notices to flues and the like so the householder knows what type and to what specification they are made.

Not-so-Key Documents

Approved Document Part L1A Conservation of Fuel and Power in New Dwellings

To be found here: http://www.planningportal.gov.uk/uploads/br/BR_PDF_ADL1A_2010.pdf or Google 'Approved Document Part L1A'.

This Approved Document claims to provide practical guidance on how to meet the energy efficiency requirements of Part 2 of the Building Regulations 2000 for new building work.

There's a general tendency in the trade to refer to Building Regulations Part L or Part J or whatever when they're talking about installations. That's not strictly accurate terminology - strictly speaking these 'Part L' and 'Part J' documents are merely 'Building Regulations Approved Documents' which explain how to interpret the Building Regulations 2000.

The only bit of Part L1A that we're interested in as woodburners is criterion 2: *The performance of the building fabric and the fixed building services should achieve reasonable overall standards of energy efficiency following the procedure set out in paragraphs 4.18 to 4.24*. Of those just paragraph 4.23 is appropriate, and that refers us back to the 'minimum efficiency' tables in the Domestic Building Services Compliance Guide!

Approved Document Part L1B Conservation of Fuel and Power in Existing Dwellings

To be found here: http://www.planningportal.gov.uk/uploads/br/BR_PDF_ADL1B_2010.pdf

Similar to Part L1A, but covering existing buildings this time, and again telling us to follow the guidance in the Domestic Building Services Compliance Guide.

And finally, as Parts J and L refer to Part F, we'd better know what it is - Approved Document Part F deals with ventilation and is available at:

http://www.planningportal.gov.uk/uploads/br/BR_PDF_ADF_2010.pdf

All this does is to refer us back to Part J for guidance as to how to provide air for fuel-burning appliances. As ever, putting the title in a search engine will find any of these documents.

CHAPTER NINE

The Renewable Heat Incentive

I'd intended to call this chapter 'Grants', but at the time of writing there are few, if any, and a declared intention by the Government to reduce the number of quasi-Government agencies. As these were traditionally the suppliers of largesse in the form of grants (the Low-Carbon Buildings Programme was a key source of cash, but was closed to new applications in May 2010), I've decided to concentrate on the most likely source of subsidies. The major source of subsidy proposed for the near future is the Renewable Heat Incentive, set up in response to targets on the UK Government to reduce the amount of CO_2 that the UK produces.

If you are viewing this as a business rather than an individual there may be other sources of funding - there certainly were up to 2010 - but these will take rather more hunting down, and are likely to have much stricter criteria than was the case in the past. Also, be aware that the Renewable Heat Incentive 'Consultation Document' of February 2010 mentions that grant money may even have to be paid back for a non-domestic installation to become eligible for Renewable Heat Incentive support. 'Further Reading' at the end of this chapter tells you where to find the latest information.

Targets

Who imposed CO_2 reduction targets on us in the first place? A combination of sources really. Most of the scientific research on worldwide climate change has been brought together under the auspices of the Inter-Governmental Panel on Climate Change (IPCC); the IPCC publishes Major Assessment Reports every few years summarising just how far up the creek we are, and in what direction we should be paddling.

These IPCC Reports - we're up to the fourth Assessment Report now, titled 'Climate Change 2007' - announce the peer-reviewed findings of the scientists, particularly climate scientists, following extensive data modeling, and amount to an interpretation of the data with as little political spin as they feel they can get away with.

The Reports go to the national Governments, and the responses to the Reports are debate, hot air, lies, spin, farcical summit meetings and finally legislation throughout the world, of varying degrees of usefulness. The legislation comes after blatantly cynical lobbying by vested interests, with the aim of diluting the original IPCC recommendations.

Because we are in the EU, that august body conducts its own review of the latest IPCC Report and produces 'Directives' binding on member states. Member states in turn produce their own legislation in response to the EU Directives; our version in the UK is the Climate Change Act 2008. It's this Act that sets the UK's legally binding targets. A few of the key provisions of this Act, verbatim from the Government's own publications, are these:

Two key aims of the Climate Change Act:

- to improve carbon management, helping the transition towards a low-carbon economy in the UK.
- to demonstrate UK leadership internationally, signaling that we are committed to taking our share of responsibility for reducing global emissions in the context of developing negotiations on a post-2012 global agreement at Copenhagen in December 2009.

Key provisions of the Act:

- A legally binding target of at least an 80 percent cut in greenhouse gas emissions by 2050, to be achieved through action in the UK and abroad. Also a reduction in emissions of at least 34 percent by 2020. Both these targets are against a 1990 baseline.

So that's what the Government says, but as potential woodburners the bit that interests us most is a sub-target. The Government has declared that: *Heat generated from renewable sources currently accounts for about 1% of total heat demand. This may need to rise to 12% to hit our binding EU targets.*

The UK Low-Carbon Transition Plan, a White Paper published in July 2009, sets out how the Government proposes to increase that percentage; one good way is deemed to be what amounts to subsidising biomass fuel to encourage us to use it. Great!

There was a consultation period during 2010 when trade associations and other interested parties were invited to respond to a set of proposals for a 'Renewable Heat Incentive', set out in a Consultation Document. It is proposed that the scheme should start in April 2011. The idea is to pay people who have biofuel systems installed a subsidy per kWh to encourage us to install.

At the time of writing there are many unresolved issues:

- It's impractical to measure how much heat you actually generate, burning woodfuel on a domestic-sized installation, so it is proposed that the subsidy be based on calculations to determine how many kWh you will use in a year. This is called 'deeming' your energy requirements, and begs a few questions, of course. I've covered 'sizing the system' in Chapter 5, but the RHI proposes to use a document called Standard Assessment Procedure 2009 (SAP 2009) to 'deem' our energy use. SAP 2009 is a bit like the data set behind the online calculators used to work out radiator and boiler size, but is massively more complex. Hopefully a simple sub-set will be used, such as the Building Research Establishment 'Standard House Set' to 'deem' your energy requirement. An extract of the Standard House Set is shown in the Table below.

- What if we buy an installation just for the subsidy and never use it? We may have a 'linked-system' and use the fossil fuel boiler to the exclusion of the woodfuel.

- The proposed inspection scheme is a potential red-tape factory. The installers are supposed to be approved under the Microgeneration Certification Scheme (MCS), but there are very few people registered at the moment - maybe that will change in response to demand, or maybe it will be a bottleneck. Hopefully the Renewable Heat Incentive will allow for members of all relevant 'competent person' schemes to be approved installers, putting some competition in there to keep prices competitive! Better still, allow a measure of DIY and offer a 'commissioning only' option by a 'competent person'.

- Recent experience with the similar 'Feed in Tariff' for renewable electricity schemes has seen installer prices rise as suppliers cash in on the increased demand. For the RHI the risk is that both installation and fuel prices may rise.

- At the consultation stage some excellent systems in terms of carbon neutrality, the big 'batch boilers', looked like being left out of the scheme as 'inefficient'. Given that the sort of scrap wood and surplus straw that they burn would otherwise rot down, this is a wrong-headed approach. From a holistic perspective these are infinitely efficient - even 10% efficiency would be better than the big fat zero that we get if no-one burns this stuff, and a good batch boiler is over 60% efficient.

- The cut-off date for existing installations to qualify for the scheme was proposed to be 15th July 2009; installations prior to that date would be ineligible. The Consultation Document proposes that installers have MCS accreditation for any scheme to qualify - does this include those installed prior to the scheme launch?

Proposed Tariffs

I've reproduced a section of the proposed tariff scale from the Consultation Document here, but must point out that whatever you are told by sales people, these figures will remain speculative until they are confirmed or changed by the Government, probably shortly before the proposed scheme comes into force in April 2011.

Tariff (proposed only) from DECC Consultation Feb 2010

Technology	Size	Tariff (pence per kWh)	Tariff Lifetime (years)
Solid Biomass	Up to 45 kW	9	15
Solid Biomass	45 - 500 kW	6.5	15

Extract from BRE Standard House Set - proposed to be used to 'deem' your energy use

Type of House	Number of Bedrooms	Floor area m2	Cavity Wall Construction kWh/yr	Solid Wall Construction kWh/yr
Mid Terrace	2	63	4699	7961
Semi-Detached	3	98	9674	16390
Detached	3	104	15774	26724

Note that the Standard House Set looks at the amount of energy the 'typical' UK house might use in a year, not the size of boiler required.

How to Calculate your Subsidy - Speculative only!

Using the two tables, the scheme would work something like this - If you have a three-bed semi-detached house with cavity walls, your 'deemed' energy use would be 9674kWh per year.

If you had a biomass boiler installed by an MCS accredited installer, and for a house of this size it would be less than a 45kW boiler (see Chapter 5 Boilers and Stoves for how to calculate boiler size), you would be paid a tariff of 9p x 9674, ie. £871 per year for a 15 year term.

The calculation makes the assumption that the tariffs set out in the consultation remain unchanged and the BRE Standard House Set figures as shown are actually used.

And Finally...

The consultation document shows a few worked examples, and to be fair, the numbers look very promising. The issues above will be resolved one way or another; if the scheme at launch is broadly as proposed, the future looks much brighter for woodburners.

Further Reading

Essential, given the changing legislation - current *Renewable Heat Incentive* documents from the Department of Energy and Climate Change (DECC). The DECC website gives the authorised versions. Other sites on the internet in late 2010 gave what appeared to be definitive information, but it was based on the the proposed tariff levels from the February 2010 Consultation Document, and was not definitive.

SAP 2009 can be found at: http://www.bre.co.uk/filelibrary/SAP/2009/SAP-2009_9-90.pdf if you want to see just how complex it is possible to make the heating requirements of a house appear if you really try.

The Author

Index

The Good Life Press Ltd.
The Old Pigsties
Clifton Fields
Lytham Road
Preston PR4 0XG
01772 633444

The Good Life Press Ltd. publishes a wide range of titles for the smallholder, 'goodlifer' and farmer. We also publish **Home Farmer,** the monthly magazine for anyone who wants to grab a slice of the good life - whether they live in the country or the city. Other titles of interest include:

A Guide to Traditional Pig Keeping by Carol Harris
An Introduction to Keeping Cattle by Peter King
Any Fool Can Be a.....Dairy Farmer by James Robertson
Any Fool Can Be a.....Pig Farmer by James Robertson
Any Fool Can Be a.....Middle Aged Downshifter by Mike Woolnough
Building and Using Your Clay Oven by Mike Rutland
Build It! by Joe Jacobs
Build It!...With Pallets by Joe Jacobs
Craft Cider Making by Andrew Lea
Making Country Wines, Ales and Cordials by Brian Tucker
Precycle! by Paul Peacock
Raising Chickens for Eggs and Meat by Mike Woolnough
Raising Goats by Felicity Stockwell
The Bread and Butter Book by Diana Sutton
The Cheese Making Book by Paul Peacock
The Frugal Life by Piper Terrett
The Polytunnel Companion by Jayne Neville
The Sausage Book by Paul Peacock
The Sheep Book for Smallholders by Tim Tyne
The Smoking and Curing Book by Paul Peacock
Worms and Wormeries by Mike Woolnough

www.goodlifepress.co.uk
www.homefarmer.co.uk

Buildng and Using Your Clay Oven

By Mike Rutland

Mike Rutland shows you how to make the ultimate architectural garden accessory – a clay oven.

Home made bread, freshly baked and still warm to serve at the BBQ; pizzas served at the kids' parties or even a slow roasted joint of lamb. All are possible with Mike's step-by-step instructions on building and using your own clay oven.

The contents include the history of the clay oven, why make and use a clay oven, the choice of materials, preparing the site for work, making the base, making and maintaining the oven and recipes including breads, pizzas and roasted meats as well as a section covering dismantling and recycling the oven at the end of its life.

And as for that slow roasted lamb – well here's the perfect recipe for you: take your joint, rub in some olive oil, stud the meat with a knife point, fill the voids made with the knife point with a piece of anchovy wrapped in a piece of rosemary and simply place it into the middle of the oven, shutting the door behind. Then simply leave it for around 3-4 hours.

The initial cooking will take place in the first half hour as the lamb "sizzles" in the heat, then, as the oven cools, the lamb will slow cook gently, the oil lubricating and the anchovies melting away into nothing more than a salty highlight. Take out the lamb, slice it thickly and serve with a good wedge of bread (cooked in the oven before the lamb, of course!) or leave it to cool and enjoy the cold cuts the next day. The lamb will not need much in the way of carving as it simply falls off the bone, making the shoulder the ideal clay oven roast as not only is it usually a pain to carve with the blade bone in the way, but it is also a hard working muscle with a good marbling of fat which will cook through and baste the meat in its own juices as it cooks slowly, helping to break down the muscle fibres to make a tender and succulent Sunday roast for those summer afternoons eating alfresco.

ISBN 978 1 90487 1 972